UNIVERSITY for BEGINNERS

First published in Australia in 2002 by
New Holland Publishers (Australia) Pty Ltd
Sydney • Auckland • London • Cape Town

14 Aquatic Drive Frenchs Forest NSW 2086 Australia
218 Lake Road Northcote Auckland New Zealand
86 Edgware Road London W2 2EA United Kingdom
80 McKenzie Street Cape Town 8001 South Africa

National Library of Australia Cataloguing-in-Publication Data:

Hardy, Elizabeth Jane, 1968 Dec. 23– .
University for beginners: the mysteries revealed.

Includes index.
ISBN 1 86436 799 7.

1. College student orientation – Australia. 2. Universities and colleges –
Australia – Handbooks, manuals, etc. 3. College students – Australia –
Life skills guides. I. Title.

378.94

Publishing Manager: Anouska Good
Project Editor: Sophie Church
Copy Editor: Susan Gray
Designer: Karlman Roper
Production Manager: Wendy Hunt
Printer: McPherson's Printing Group

10 9 8 7 6 5 4 3 2 1

UNIVERSITY for BEGINNERS

the mysteries revealed!

DR ELIZABETH HARDY

NEW HOLLAND

For Audrey Hardy and Richard Hardy,
my first and most important teachers.

ABOUT THE AUTHOR

Dr Elizabeth Hardy loves university so much she has never actually left. She holds a Bachelor of Arts, Diplomas in Journalism and Information and Library Studies, and a PhD in Literature. She has recently moved from the University of Western Australia, Perth, to the University of Queensland, Brisbane, where she is working on the national literary database AustLit. She has encountered hundreds of panicky first-year students during a decade spent at uni ... this book is the result.

CONTENTS

INTRODUCTION:

ROLLER-COASTER OR LUXURY CRUISE? WHAT TO EXPECT FROM YOUR UNIVERSITY EXPERIENCE

University will probably change your life forever, and in a number of ways.

You may have just won a place in the course of your choice, or may still be thinking about taking the plunge into tertiary study. You might be entering university straight from school, or be returning to study after some time in the workforce. Whatever your situation, the secrets of university life will probably initially seem like an unsolvable puzzle. To the anxious outsider, it is a world of mystery that resists understanding. The mission of this book is to show you that you don't have to just run blindly into the arcane world of tertiary study. It offers a thorough explanation of what to expect in your first year at university, and how to handle a range of situations you may never have faced before.

The book is divided into two parts. Part One: The Secrets of Successful Study covers everything you need to know about elementary academic skills. It will explain the basics of essay writing, research, exams and tutorials. But the university experience affects many different aspects of your life. This is why Part Two: Student Survival Skills discusses a range of practical issues, from money management to making new friends and handling stress.

WHAT WILL UNIVERSITY BE LIKE?

In the lead-up to your first semester, you've probably been on the receiving end of countless lectures about the importance of a tertiary education —the advantages it gives you, the opportunities it represents. You may have heard phrases like 'golden opportunity' and 'chance of a lifetime'.

Well, believe it or not, while this advice may be irritating in the extreme, it's also absolutely right. A university education can transform your life.

But even though starting university is a huge and exciting step, many new students feel that entering the university world for the first time is a bit like landing on a different planet without the proper supplies or equipment.

I found my first day at university frankly terrifying. I can clearly remember wandering around the campus feeling lost, confused and very unsure about what was expected of me. Believe me, I've been right where you are now—standing anxiously at the threshold of some intense learning experiences.

But after a shaky start I discovered that university offered me things I couldn't get anywhere else. Where else can you have regular contact with great teachers who are often leaders in their fields? How else can you be exposed to so many new and mind-blowing ideas that your head starts to swim? And where else will you meet hundreds of people who share your interests?

It doesn't matter which course you've chosen; you've also signed up for the roller-coaster ride of your life. If you approach your time at university with an open mind and a sense of excitement, you'll graduate with something even better than improved job prospects and a degree to hang on your wall. You'll have made some lifelong friends, expanded your understanding of the world, and engaged with a range of fascinating ideas and theories. And you'll have shown yourself—and everyone else—what you're capable of achieving. By the time you step off the roller-coaster back onto solid ground, you'll be wiser and intellectually richer. You'll have made contact with a whole new world of knowledge and skills which you could never have accessed without first climbing into that roller-coaster car.

But at this stage, you probably still feel nervous about the experience which awaits you. You now have two choices: if you're worried about a particular aspect of university life, read the table of contents and skip ahead to the appropriate chapter to put your fears to rest; if you feel a generalised sense of anxiety, settle back and prepare to be reassured by the practical and realistic advice you're about to find in the pages which follow.

Enjoy the ride!

THE FIVE SECRETS TO UNIVERSITY SUCCESS

How can you maximise your chances of getting the most out of university and actually *enjoying* the next few years? These are the five key pieces of information I wish someone had told me before I turned up for my first day on campus. Most people have to learn these secrets by trial and error, so mastering the following concepts now will put you way ahead in the race to graduation.

The First Secret: University will change who you are.

No matter which degree you've enrolled in, a lot of bold new ideas are lying in wait for you. Keep an open mind, and expect to have your current way of thinking challenged. It's very likely that, by the time you graduate, you won't be the same person you are now. You'll see yourself and the world very differently because you've had the chance to view a range of different realities and perspectives.

The Second Secret: Your level of success at university is entirely up to you.

If you've just finished school, you may be used to having teachers keeping tabs on your progress and checking to see how much work you're doing from day to day. If you've been in the workforce for a while, you'll have got into the habit of reporting to a boss. But once you enter the university world, no-one will be gently reminding you to finish your homework or do a bit more reading. On Planet University, the days of forging long-term alliances with favourite teachers or flexible employers are over. It's up to you to decide whether you'll succeed or fail at university. No-one else will be taking responsibility for your results, so self-motivation is absolutely essential from day one. (We'll talk about how to stay motivated later on, in Chapter 7.)

The Third Secret: Good organisation will get you further than a huge IQ.

No matter how smart you are, it's crucial to be well organised at university. If you make it a priority to manage your time as well as your information, you'll be able to keep track of the many different tasks you'll have to juggle on a day-to-day basis. Being on top of issues like where your lecture notes are, and the dates of your exams, can often mean the difference between passing and failing. It won't matter how intelligent you are if you forget to hand in your assignments on time and can't remember which exam room you're supposed to be in!

The Fourth Secret: Prepare to meet some key players in your future.
Some of the people you come into contact with over the next few years (and maybe even in the next few weeks!) will probably end up playing starring roles in your life. You may meet your future life partner outside a lecture theatre. You may end up impressing a tutor who recommends you for your dream job. The possibilities for connecting with important, or just plain interesting, people in the university environment are virtually unlimited. Be aware that every day you're swimming in a social pool filled to overflowing with potential new friends and acquaintances.

The Fifth Secret: Sometimes university is harder than you expected.
Be prepared to be challenged in ways you didn't know existed. There will probably be moments in which you feel overwhelmed and begin to doubt that you are cut out to get a degree. In these darker moments, remember that this response is completely normal! Everyone feels anxious and uncertain from time to time. Don't ever assume that these feelings are proof that you can't make the grade. When the going gets tough, hang in there. You'll be amazed at what you can achieve with a bit of persistence and the right support.

PART ONE:
THE SECRETS OF
SUCCESSFUL STUDY

1. WHAT HAPPENS IN A LECTURE?

Lectures tend to be a mixed bag. Sometimes time will fly and your hand will start to ache as you scribble down the fascinating ideas flowing around you. At other times, you will be convinced that time has stopped and that you must have been sitting in the lecture hall for several hours. During these latter moments, it's a good idea to stifle your yawns and try to look alert. It will make a better impression on the lecturer, and give you something to do in between glancing at your watch.

WHAT IS A LECTURE?

A lecture is a measured dose of information about a particular topic. In most units, there will be a set number of lectures held per week. Lectures tend to contain all the information that will appear in the end-of-semester exam, so it's vital that you try to make it to most of them.

The order of events goes something like this. The students gather in the designated lecture room or theatre, preferably arriving a few minutes before the beginning of the lecture. When the lecturer turns up, he or she will stand at the front of the room and deliver a prepared talk about one aspect of the unit. Sometimes you will have one or two lecturers for a unit, and sometimes several, as different academics contribute their specialist knowledge to the course.

Academics come in a range of personality types, so some of your lectures will be delivered by natural performers who will make you really think about the material, while other lecturers will have a more reserved style, perhaps making it harder to concentrate. The challenge is to get something valuable out of every lecture, regardless of the academic's style of delivery.

WHAT'S EXPECTED OF YOU?

First of all, you're expected to make it to the lecture on time. There's no surer way of getting the lecturer off-side than turning up late, clambering over people to obtain a seat, and then noisily going through your bag to get out your notebook and find your pens. If you try this approach to attending lectures, be warned: many lecturers won't hesitate to publicly embarrass you as payback for interrupting them. And after a dressing-down in public, it can be very difficult to dredge up any enthusiasm for the remainder of the course.

You'll need to bring along the proper tools for the lecture. A notebook or lecture pad, and a couple of pens in case one runs out, are a good start. A pencil or two doesn't hurt either. Bring too much paper rather than too little—it's *really annoying* if you run out of paper and have to just sit there as the lecturer tells you vital information about the exam! If you prefer to take notes on a laptop computer, make sure that you have enough battery power to make it through the lecture. Bring a notebook as back-up just in case. Lecturers will never fail to surprise you with how much information they can cram into a short period of time.

Once the lecture gets under way, don't talk; listen. It can be really tempting to carry on a whispered conversation with an interesting person you've just met, but rest assured that the lecturer will notice. Once again, you're setting yourself up for some serious public humiliation. Offended lecturers have been known to stop the lecture and wait for the chatting students to notice that 300 people are now staring at them. Other common humiliations include being told to leave and having to pack up your things in front of a large, impatient student audience, or being given detailed and pointed directions to the coffee shop, with the observation that it might be a better place for a conversation. If this ever happens to you, you'd better hope that this lecturer is not also your tutor. Your tutor marks your assignments, and it's a bad, bad plan to annoy the people who determine your grades.

But by far the best way to drive a lecturer crazy is to leave your mobile phone on. If it rings in the middle of a lecture, be afraid—be very afraid. The horror stories arising from this situation are many. One infuriated lecturer stopped talking mid-sentence, walked over to the cringing student and answered her ringing phone. He calmly let her caller know that he was speaking to the lecturer and that the student was currently unavailable. Humiliations of these kinds take place while everyone in the course has a good laugh. Save yourself from the embarrassment and get into the habit of turning off your phone before you enter the lecture room.

Where you sit in the lecture theatre will make a difference to how much you learn, and the impression you make on the lecturer. If you sit up the back of the theatre, you'll very often be surrounded by latecomers and students who are there to catch up with their mates rather than take notes. It's pretty hard to learn anything from back there, and the lecturer will either not see you or will assume you're not taking the course seriously.

It's a much better idea to sit nearer the front. You don't have to sit in the very first row, but somewhere in the first third of the room is ideal. It's easier to concentrate there, and much less tempting to chat during the lecture, seeing you'll be in full view of the lecturer. Being visible like this can also offer another advantage: if you go to most of the lectures (and pay attention and take notes), the lecturer will get to know your face and will notice you're a regular. Academics love to see students making a genuine effort to learn. Then, if you need help later on in the course, or an extension on an assignment, the lecturer will have registered you're serious about the unit and will be more likely to cut you some slack.

HOW DO YOU TAKE LECTURE NOTES?

At your very first lecture for each unit you may get a list of recommended reading for future lectures. In general, it's not expected that you'll read every single thing on this list. But if you can read one or two of the articles or chapters on the lecture reading list—*before* the lecture—you'll have a much better understanding of what the lecturer's talking about. The basic concepts of the topic will not be completely new to you.

And because you'll be familiar with key terms and the main issues, it'll be easier to work out what's important enough to note down. When you turn up to a lecture without having done any reading, it's considerably more difficult to know what you should write in your notes. Sometimes everything seems important but it's physically impossible to capture each one of the lecture's points.

However, there will be some clear cues. The lecturer may use an overhead projector or give a Powerpoint presentation as part of the lecture. The information that appears on the screen or overheads is probably important, especially if it's in point or list form. Write it down.

Some academics provide lecture notes as handouts at the beginning of the lecture. Many students make a grab for these handouts and then hang out up the back and have a chat, thinking all the work's been done for them. Some even arrive at the lecture hall, pick up the notes and head straight for the coffee shop without bothering to sit through the lecture. They've just walked straight into a very common trap (most probably invented by an academic with a sadistic sense of humour): in most cases, lecture notes offer only a skeleton outline of the subject being discussed. Sure, they're useful as a summary of the issues, but you'll almost certainly need to flesh them out yourself as the lecture progresses.

Note-taking gets easier with practice. Get down what you can and fill in the gaps by reading the recommended articles, or by asking your lecturer for advice.

AUDIO TAPES AND WEB-BASED LECTURES

Your lectures may be taped by the lecturer and then later made available in a media lab. Your lecturer will let you know if this is the case. Some students prefer to tape the lectures themselves, using a portable tape-recorder which they set up at the front of the lecture hall. If you want to do this, make sure you get the lecturer's permission first.

Bear in mind that you shouldn't rely solely on tapes of lectures instead of your own lecture notes. Whether you listen to the tapes in the media lab or at home, you'll need to factor in the extra time it will take to listen to, and take notes from, the tapes. Will you actually have time to do this? This method entails sitting through the lecture again, and so effectively doubles the number of hours per week you're spending in lectures.

Another danger which lurks in this method is that it's very easy to let the tapes pile up week after week and never quite get around to listening to them. A stack of tapes may contain a semester's worth of lectures, but you need to transcribe them to get to the information they contain. A pile of tapes and no notes are utterly useless when exams are just around the corner.

Some lecturers provide copies of their lecture notes on the web, usually through the home page of the relevant department. If you can't make it to all the lectures, these notes can be worth their weight in gold.

However, like the audio-tape method, it's also very easy to put off checking the lecture notes on the web for weeks at a time, and then suddenly realise you have to print out and read six weeks' worth of lectures before you can start to write your assignments!

FIVE WAYS TO TAME YOUR LECTURE NOTES

Lecture notes have a mysterious tendency to turn into an unruly pile of papers, covered in strange scribblings that soon lose their meaning. Here's how to make sure that the time and effort you put into taking notes in lectures doesn't go to waste.

1. REVIEW YOUR LECTURE NOTES THE SAME DAY.

Make sure you understand all the issues discussed in the lecture, and that you have a firm grip on the information you've just learned. Having a sense of clarity early on will make it easier to recall that knowledge when it's time to write about it in assignments and exams.

2. MAKE SURE YOUR NOTES ARE LEGIBLE.

You'll need to be able to read your notes again for assignments, and in preparation for the exam. If there are parts that are difficult to read, or written in a form of shorthand you've just invented, write them out or type them up while you still remember what those little symbols mean. If you can't make sense of your lecture notes later on, it was pretty much a waste of time going to the lecture.

3. SET UP A FILING SYSTEM AND USE IT.

Lecture notes are no use to you if they're scrunched up in a corner of your study, or have fallen into the black hole behind your desk. It's essential to use a filing system so that you can get your hands on the notes for each lecture you've attended, whenever you need to.

Once your lecture notes are in a legible format, file the notes for different units in week order, in lever-arch files, one for each unit. Coloured file dividers also make it easier to quickly access the section you're looking for, with subdivisions for each topic in the unit. Make sure each set of lecture notes contains the week number, the title of the lecture, the date and the lecturer's name. This makes it that much easier if you're asking for help later on. You can then say in your tutorial, 'Can we talk about the three main points of Dr Maxwell's lecture on Shelley given in Week 3?' This method allows you to be specific and focused.

An effective filing system will add ten years to your life in terms of eliminated stress. When it's time to start assignments and study for exams, you can be understandably smug as you open your files and find the exact information you want in a matter of seconds.

4. THINK TWICE BEFORE YOU LEND YOUR LECTURE NOTES.

The notes you take in lectures represent a huge investment of time and effort on your part. It's no mean feat to go to a whole semester's worth of lectures and painstakingly take notes. So be very careful about automatically lending them to anyone who happened to miss some lectures. It's very easy to lose track of your notes, and it can be a real nightmare to get them back once you've given them away. Borrowed lecture notes have a habit of being loaned to friends of friends who also missed the lecture. These people in their turn always seem to know of someone else in need, so they may pass them on again. If you never see your notes again, you've wasted your time going to the lecture yourself. And you may end up in court for assault if you discover that the person you initially lent them to has passed them to their housemate's cousin's brother, and has no way of getting them back to you before the exam!

If you'd like to help out a friend by lending them your notes, by all means go with them and find a photocopier and have them make a copy. But don't let your notes out of your sight unless you're absolutely sure they'll be returned to you—quickly, and preferably without coffee spilled all over them!

5. LOOK AFTER YOUR NOTES.

It's also very unwise to leave your notes lying around campus. You might think your wallet or laptop are the worst things you could lose if your bag is stolen, but at least those things and their contents are largely replaceable. If you lose a whole year's worth of notes, however, you'll also have lost a year's worth of work! This is a disturbing situation to find yourself in when exams are approaching. So take your notes with you when you go to lunch or to the coffee shop. Smile at your friends when they call you paranoid— when they have *their* notes stolen, they may see things differently.

FOUR GOOD REASONS FOR ATTENDING LECTURES

If you're not studying externally and can get to most of the lectures in the flesh, here are four good reasons why you should go out of your way to make it to as many of them as you can:

1. A lecture is where you get the all-important handouts that contain essential information like required reading, details of tutorial times, a week-by-week outline of the course topics, due dates for assignments and information on how the unit is assessed. If you don't get hold of these, you'll be in the dark all semester.

2. If you have any questions about any aspect of the course, you can approach the lecturer at the end of the lecture and get an immediate response to your query. This can help to establish a working relationship that could be really beneficial, particularly if you end up majoring in the subject and working with the lecturer over the next few years.

3. Attending a lecture in person really increases your chances of paying attention to the material, and taking the information on board. Remember, this is a topic you've chosen to learn about, so you may as well listen and make the most of the new information.

4. This is a great opportunity to get to know some of the other people in your course. Think about it: you're in a room with dozens, possibly hundreds, of other people who share an interest with you. Most of them are feeling as uncertain as you are, so take the initiative and say hello to someone sitting near you (though only before or after the lecture). You may start a new friendship or, at the very least, connect with someone you can talk about the course with. It never hurts to have an ally or two in all your units.

2. WHAT ARE TUTORIALS?

Tutorials (also known as 'tutes') are regular, compulsory meetings in which a group of students get together with a tutor to discuss course material. Tutorials are usually designed to complement lectures, giving you a chance to thrash out some of the issues raised in the lectures. The discussion that takes place in a tute is often fairly informal, making it a great setting for tossing around ideas and asking questions about anything that had you baffled in the most recent lecture.

Normally you'll hear about the details of tute times and locations in the first lecture for each unit. It's a good idea to find the relevant tutorial room—and the list that's probably pinned up on the wall outside it—as soon as possible. Get your name down on this list and register your interest in the tutorial time that suits you, as the most convenient tutes always get filled first. Unless you want all your tutes to start at 8am or 8pm, get in quick!

WHAT'S EXPECTED OF YOU?

Lists of lecture and tutorial topics are supplied at the beginning of the semester. Often this information includes details of articles and books that are considered recommended reading for each topic. It's expected that you will have read at least some of the assigned items before your tute each week.

As you do your preparation reading each week, take brief notes which cover the main points of the article or chapter. These notes can act as prompts later on during the tute, so that you can remember the finer points of what you've read and contribute to the discussion. Another useful technique is to note down any questions which come to mind as you read. Raise these in the tute, and see if any other students can shed light on the issues, based on their own preparation.

The key difference between a lecture and a tutorial is simple: at lectures you *take* notes, at tutes you *bring* notes.

It's important to attend all tutorials, but it's *especially* important to get to the first tutorial for each of your units. This is where you hear about the vital stuff: course requirements, how things will be assessed, and when the assignments are due. If you miss out on this information you can spend all semester trying to work out what's due—and when!

Some tutors like to start the first tute with an ice-breaking exercise. This involves getting everyone to say something very basic about why they're at university, and what else they're studying. You might think tutors do this for the fun of making new students squirm, but in fact this approach has its uses. The ice-breaker gets the members of the group chatting to each other, and also helps you to find out the names and interests of your fellow students. After the ice is broken, your tutor will expect everybody to contribute to the group discussion, and may ask you directly for your ideas on that week's topic.

WHAT IF YOU DON'T DO THE READING BEFORE THE TUTE?

It's amazingly common for first-year students to believe that they can outwit their tutors—a couple of jokes and the odd knowledgable 'mmm' of agree-ment and the tutor will never know they're not prepared. In fact, it's a pretty good bet that your tutor will take in the region of six seconds to see through this sophisticated ploy. (Tutors were once students themselves, remember!)

Tutors have heard every excuse ever invented. They're trained to spot a faker at 50 paces and they *will* notice if you try and sidetrack the tutorial discussion onto a 'more interesting' topic. Your average tutor will soon cotton on to the fact that you haven't done the required reading, and this doesn't make a great impression. Often your participation in tutes counts towards your final mark, so it's a good idea to not only turn up regularly, but also to try to contribute something of value to the discussion. You can do this by coming to grips with some of the set reading—and reading even one article is better than nothing at all.

BUT WHAT IF YOU'RE TOO NERVOUS TO SPEAK?

There's no doubt that sometimes it can be a bit daunting to join in a group discussion, especially if you don't know anyone else in the group. But it's a strange fact that the longer you leave it, the harder it is to speak up in a tute. Force yourself to ask a question or make a comment. There are lots of ways to make this easier for yourself: look at your notes and see if you need any points clarified; think back to the lecture and ask yourself whether you understood the gist of what was said; or try coming up with a couple of questions while you're doing the reading. Ask one of them near the beginning of the tute, rather than sitting there trying to pluck up the courage to speak.

Some tutors make a point of asking the silent students for their opinions, so take the initiative and make a contribution before you're put on the spot with a curly question you may not be able to answer. Get into this habit from the start and you're likely to not only get more out of tutes but to make a better impression on your tutor. Being active in tutes leads directly to better marks and a more compassionate response if you ever need to ask your tutor for an extension, or for help with an assignment.

TUTORIAL PRESENTATIONS AND HOW TO SURVIVE THEM

Sometimes part of the assessment for a course will involve giving a tutorial presentation. This essentially means that each student presents a prepared talk to the rest of the tute group, on a topic related directly to the course. The student will then submit to the tutor a written paper on the subject, which will be marked and included as part of the final assessment. Some departments expect you to present a tutorial paper right from the word go; others wait until you hit second or third year. Either way, it's pretty much inevitable that giving a presentation will form part of your assessment at some stage.

Although giving a tute presentation might sound like a scary prospect, it is in fact an opportunity to pick up a valuable skill you'll draw on throughout your life.

Before we get into the nitty-gritty of giving a paper, here's some little-known insider information about tute presentations: *everyone gets nervous before giving a talk*. That motormouth who never shuts up in your tute, the loudest person in the coffee shop, even a good proportion of your lecturers—they all get butterflies before they take centre stage. There's nothing wrong with you if you feel nervous, and there are plenty of things you can do about it.

So what *can* you do to overcome feelings of fear? The best way is to prepare very well for your presentation. If you're really nervous about the prospect of giving a talk, it can be tempting to put it out of your mind until you absolutely have to think about it—like five minutes before the tute! This game plan guarantees that the talk will actually be a *more* traumatic experience than it might otherwise have been, because there's no way you'll be ready to discuss the subject. A better approach is to face your fear by tackling the topic as soon as possible and making sure you have a really thorough understanding of it. You'll feel much more confident if you know what you're talking about.

Write your paper well in advance of presenting it, if possible, and practice reading it aloud. Some people just refer to notecards and don't read the paper word for word. If this method works for you, great—do it that way. Otherwise, it's perfectly acceptable to read your paper out in the tute. If you rehearse well in advance, you get the chance to find out in private which presentation style makes you most comfortable.

As you practise your paper, make sure you time your presentation. It can be pretty embarrassing to finish giving your paper 20 minutes early (although you'll probably win popularity contests with the other students if the tute ends early!). The average tute presentation is expected to be approximately 30 minutes—not (usually) the length of the entire tute, as often there will be a short discussion after your paper.

If you practise your paper several times until you're happy with its content and delivery, you'll end up almost learning the material word for word. You'll be so familiar with what you want to say that you'll be much less likely to be paralysed by fear in the tute. The rehearsal stage also helps you to get used to hearing your own voice out loud—this can be strange until you get used to it.

On the day of your presentation, turn up to the tute a couple of minutes early so you don't feel rushed, and check that your papers are in order. Smile and stay positive when other people inevitably ask you if you're nervous. If you answer, 'I'm really freaking out and I don't think I can do it', you'll convince yourself this is true. There's absolutely no need to panic. Usually, it'll all be over in less than 30 minutes.

Before the tute begins, and while you're being introduced, take a couple of deep breaths. Remind yourself of how well prepared you are. Try to relax your body, and don't worry about stopping to breathe deeply while giving your talk if your throat seems to have tightened up. You may be offered a glass of water at the beginning of the tute, so take a sip when you need it.

Try to remember to make eye contact with the other members of the group as you're presenting your paper. If you look up and around the room as you're talking, it conveys the idea that you're trying to communicate your ideas to the group, rather than just talking to yourself. Bringing other tute members into the discussion can also help you to feel you're not standing on your own, centre-stage in the spotlight. Ask leading questions like, 'Did anyone else find that?' or, 'Has anyone got any comment on that?'.

Make a conscious effort to slow down. When people get nervous they tend to speak more quickly. Force yourself to pause at important points and let your audience take in what you're saying. You've put in a lot of effort to get to this point—you may as well make sure that everyone understands what you have to say! A couple of extra seconds here and there can really enhance your presentation.

At the end of your presentation you may be required to answer some questions on the content of your paper. Stay calm and focused and continue to breathe deeply. Listen closely to the questions and give yourself a few moments to consider your answers.

And when the presentation is over; reward yourself! Don't agonise over whether every word was perfect or whether people understood all of your points. Your presentation is finished; you can't change it now. Congratulate yourself on confronting what for most people is a daunting task. Buy yourself a present, go to a movie you've been meaning to see, have a drink with some friends. At the very least, make sure you take the rest of the day off and relax: you've just survived a tute presentation!

HOW TO MAKE YOUR TUTOR HATE YOU: EIGHT THINGS **NOT** *TO DO IN A TUTORIAL*

Here's a quick run-down of what *not* to do in tutorials. Remember: your tutors usually have the power to decide your final mark for each unit. If you catch yourself indulging in any of the behaviours described below, check yourself *before* you gain a powerful enemy.

1. DON'T start preparing for the tutorial in the five minutes spent waiting outside the tute room. Once the tute begins, it will be painfully obvious that: a) the corridor wasn't such a great place to do the reading, and b) it takes more than five minutes to get to grips with the issues to be discussed.

2. If you've done no reading whatsoever, DON'T try to replace intelligent responses with charm and wit. The tutor can pick this technique a mile away, and knows that the person who keeps leading the discussion off onto unrelated topics probably hasn't been near a book lately. Sadistic tutors might ask, 'Who hasn't done the reading?' and then look around the room to see who's squirming. Usually, it's less hassle to just do some preparation.

3. DON'T grill your tutors about their qualifications and experience in the first tutorial. Chances are your tutors know what they're talking about (that's why they're getting paid to pass on their knowledge of the subject). Challenging their authority and credibility—particularly in front of the other students—will mark you in their minds as a likely

troublemaker. If you *do* demand to know the tutor's credentials, you should plan to hand in superb, flawless work. Offended tutors are notoriously ruthless when it comes to marking assignments.

4. DON'T sit with your head down and scribble furiously throughout the tute. Avoiding eye contact won't always save you from answering questions. And, if the 'tute notes' you're taking are filled with little cubes in 3-D or hearts and flowers, you may be really unlucky and get to display your work to the rest of the group at the tutor's request.

5. DON'T award yourself an extension on an assignment without checking with your tutor. Plenty of students hand papers in days or even weeks late, without ever being granted a formal extension. This strategy can seriously endanger your survival in the course. Some departments won't accept late work at all, while others impose severe penalties, knocking off marks for every day the assignment is late. Always ring or email the tutor and explain the need for an extension *before* the due date. Remember, most tutors are only merciless if you deliberately provoke them.

6. DON'T harass tutors about how long they'll take to mark your assignments—particularly if you've only just submitted the work. Bear in mind that your tutor is probably teaching in more than one course and is likely to be facing up to two weekends' worth of essay marking anyway. This prospect is enough to put anyone in a bad mood. So be tactful, patient, and don't nag.

7. DON'T arrive late or attempt to leave early. The more reckless latecomer will take five minutes to unpack his bags and then interrupt the discussion to ask what he's missed. Five minutes before the tute is due to end, he'll snap his books shut and noisily start packing up. It doesn't bother him that someone else may still be

talking. He'll shift around impatiently, sigh loudly, roll his eyes and generally make it clear that he's ready to be somewhere else. As you can imagine, this isn't a winning move.

8. DON'T leave your phone on when the tute starts. And, if the worst-case scenario comes about and the phone starts ringing in the middle of a tute discussion, *never* actually take the call. And no, it doesn't help if you leave the room to talk and then come back in when the conversation is over!

3. WHAT EXACTLY DO THEY MEAN BY 'RESEARCH'?

By now you'll have found your way to some lectures and be well into the note-taking groove. You'll have survived the getting-to-know-you games of your first tutes and begun to engage with the material in your course. But just when you're starting to think you're on top of this university game, BANG! You get your first list of assignment questions.

How do you choose a question, and how do you find out enough about your topic to write about it?

WHERE DO YOU START?

The first thing to do is to choose your question from the list given out in the lecture or tutorial. Don't decide which one to answer right away. One or two may 'jump out' at you if they address your favourite area of the course or one of your ongoing interests, but read all the questions a couple of times before you decide. Choose the right one from the beginning so that you don't make the horrifying discovery later on that you should have picked a different question. (By the way, your choice of question doesn't have to conform with your friends' choice, nor with general speculation about which questions may be easier or harder. Choose the question you're genuinely interested in, that *you* want to answer.)

Spend some time getting to know your question. Focus on what it's actually asking you. Do you understand all the terms? Are you clear about what you're being asked to do? If you're the slightest bit confused about *any* aspect of your chosen question, go and see your tutor *before* you spend two weeks researching this topic. If you don't fully understand the question, you won't be able to answer it properly.

Of course, chances are you already know something about the subject you've chosen to write about, since your essay or assignment questions will relate directly to the subjects discussed in lectures and tutes. So, ideally, you will have already done some reading on them. Go straight to the recommended reading lists you've already received for your chosen topic. The items on these lists are useful starting points, and are usually accessible and reader-friendly for new students. These reading lists are the logical place to start your research.

FIRST STOP: THE LIBRARY

In the first few weeks of semester you'll notice fliers posted around the library advertising a free library-orientation tour. This may sound like a pretty boring invitation, but it's actually a very wise move to accept. In just an hour or so you'll be shown the basics of how to use the catalogue and be led around the different sections of the library. You'll also be given information about how to borrow items from your own and other university libraries. Your university may also have smaller, specialist libraries which you may be directed to. You'll learn how to use these libraries as well.

Most of the material on your recommended reading lists may be available in a section of the library known as the Reserve Collection, or Closed Reserve. Generally, you can borrow the items in Reserve for a couple of hours at a time (check the specifics with your own library). This gives you enough time to look through the book and either take notes or photocopy the relevant passages of a chapter to read later on.

The items on your reading list can also lead you to other relevant research material. Look in the back of the recommended books, in their bibliographies. Some of these items will be helpful to your own research. Check the titles: do any of them seem to be directly relevant to your essay question? What about author names: has your tutor already told you who the key writers in your area are?

It's also an idea to check publication dates of potential research material. Think about whether you need the latest information, or if older books may be just as adequate. If you're looking for more information about a specific event, you'll obviously want to narrow your search to articles and books published after that date.

MEET THE CATALOGUE

Armed with your research leads, spend some time at the library catalogue, which will invariably be available on a computer. Read the introductory screen and familiarise yourself with the catalogue layout. You'll see that you can search the catalogue for material in the library using different methods—by title, author, subject or key word.

For example, click on 'title search' and enter the exact title of a book from your reading list. If the library holds the book, the catalogue will tell you the call number of the item, and where it is in the library. A call number is a combination of numbers and letters on the spine label of every item in the library. The numbers reflect a book's place in a subject-based system of organisation.

Note down the title of the book and its call number. Most libraries display maps to each floor which direct you to the appropriate area for the call number you're after. Take your time and get to know your way around. Before long, you'll know where the 300s are, and whether the 900s are on the third floor or the first floor, for example.

When searching the catalogue for a journal article, do a title search and enter the title of the *journal*, not the title of the article. The catalogue will tell you which volumes of the journal the library holds. You then need to go to the shelf, find the appropriate volume and use the table of contents to direct you to the right article. Easier still, your recommended reading list, or the bibliography you're using, will provide you with the specific page numbers.

THE DIFFERENCE BETWEEN REFERENCES TO BOOKS AND REFERENCES TO ARTICLES

This one's easy.

On your reading list or in a bibliography, a reference to a book looks like this: Wood, Denis. *The Power of Maps*. London: Routledge, 1993.

A reference to an article looks like this: Wallace, Mike. 'Mickey Mouse History: Portraying the Past at Disney World.' *Radical History Review*, vol. 32, 1985, pp. 33–57.

In either case, the part in italics (sometimes it's underlined instead) is the part you look up in the catalogue.

YOU'VE FOUND WHAT YOU NEED: WHAT NEXT?

Before long, you'll be sitting at your desk surrounded by a pile of unread research material. Rule number one is, don't panic! You're not expected to read *everything* ever written about your subject. The secret is to target your reading so that you absorb enough information to answer your assignment question effectively. There are two quick ways of doing this:

1. Open one of the books and look firstly in the index at the back, and then at the table of contents at the front. Do you recognise any key words in your subject, or important names in the field? Those are the pages to start reading first.

2. If you're faced with a *huge* chapter in a book, find out how much of it you need to read by skimming through it first. Start at the beginning of the chapter, read the introduction and check the subheadings. Read the sections under the relevant subheadings and the chapter conclusion to determine whether you need to read the entire chapter. It often helps to read the introduction and conclusion of the book as well as the chapter.

Of course, the more you read, the more you'll learn, but you'll probably be reading for more than one essay or assignment at a time. So bear in mind that you have to manage your research in order to learn enough about each topic you'll be writing on.

SMART NOTE-TAKING

When taking notes from the relevant reading material, don't bother copying out whole passages. It's not only a waste of time, but if you include that kind of thing in your essay you're committing the most heinous crime possible on Planet University: plagiarism. Copying other people's words or ideas can result in getting a fail grade for your essay, and it may even cause you to get kicked out of university altogether. It's a much better idea to read a passage, think about it and summarise it in your own words, as you understand it.

If you feel that a direct quote from the author would add punch to your assignment, make sure you enclose the quoted words in quotation marks and note the source in your essay (see pp. 43–44).

Each time you start to take notes from a new source, ensure that you write the details of that source at the top of your page of notes, including everything you'll need for your bibliography. (See Chapter 4: Essay-writing made easy, for more about bibliographies and a fuller definition of plagiarism.) It's also useful to note down the page number you're summarising in the margin of your notebook (or your document if you're typing it). This way you can give specific, detailed references to your sources when you touch on these ideas in your essays.

THE FOUR DEADLY SINS OF RESEARCH

The thought of having to do research shouldn't hang over you like a terrifying ghoul. The research process doesn't have to be intimidating, and it doesn't have to consume all your available time and energy. If you hate doing research, chances are you're committing one of the following deadly sins. See if you recognise your approach in any of these less-than-effective research methods.

1. Leaving research to the last minute.

Even if you target your sources so that you look at only the most relevant items, the fact remains that you can't research an essay in half an hour.

Start as soon as you get the questions. This way, you can find the information you need steadily—and you can access the books you need before everyone else has already checked them out of the library!

2. Reading and reading, until you're totally confused, and drowning under waves of information.

Be selective about what you read, and make a start on an essay draft as soon as you have a handle on the subject. You can always top up your reading and improve your draft with extra information and missing facts later on.

3. Getting sidetracked by irrelevant information.

Stick firmly to the topic you're researching. When you begin reading, it can be tempting to wander down research avenues that may be fascinating but are completely unrelated to your assignment question. This is even more likely to happen if you're not particularly interested in your research topic. Discipline yourself to stay on track and focus on the 'question at hand. If you're genuinely interested in this distracting subject, make a note of the bibliographical details of the relevant book or journal, and get back to reading it *after* you've handed in your essay.

4. Relying solely on the internet for your information.

To a panicking student who hasn't done enough research, the internet shimmers like an information oasis in the desert. There seem to be so many advantages of using the net to research an essay: the information is available when the library is closed; and you can download and print out page upon page of data. However, the internet is more likely to be a research mirage than an source of reliable information.

For a start, much of the material on the net cannot be verified. It is often long out of date and based on very old scholarship. Gorgeous graphics can mask some suspect 'information' which may have been posted by someone who claims to be an expert on the given subject, but in fact has no qualifications and is simply putting up web pages devoted to his or her latest hobby or interest. Be very, very careful about basing the bulk of your research on what you find online. At university, you're much more likely to be rewarded for using sources that can be verified, and which have been published in reputable journals and books.

4. ESSAY-WRITING MADE EASY

Essays are a basic element of assessment in many university courses. There's a very high probability that you will write many, many essays during your time on Planet University. University-style essays are quite different from the ones you wrote at school, and from the kind of writing you'll have come across in the workplace. An academic essay has several recognisable features. Write an essay that takes all of these into account and you'll be well on your way to a decent mark.

When you've finished your research and feel you have a thorough grasp of the subject, it's time to work out what you want to say and how you want to say it. Make up an essay plan before you start writing by listing your major points and sketching the proposed structure of your essay.

THE DESIGNING STAGE: THE ESSAY PLAN

Before you start writing your essay, you must have a thorough understanding of the shape and form it will take. It is impossible to construct a convincing argument without a plan. Start by noting down the main points of your essay, based on what you've discovered in your research. Your essay question sheet will specify a required word limit, which will usually restrict you to no more than two or three main points. Don't try to cram the entire history of your subject into 1500 words.

Once you've chosen those two or three main points, think about which order to present them in. Is there a linear, developing logic to your points, which will move your essay forward and progress your argument? Think about how to arrange the material to support your message.

After you've settled on the content and order of the ideas which comprise the body of your essay, spend some time planning the introduction and conclusion. Don't lead your reader through a series of twists and turns, and then reveal your main points with a flourish just before the end. Spell things out, right from the start. This is a mark of a well-conceived and organised essay. Similarly, invest some time thinking about what to include in your conclusion.

HOW TO BUILD AN ESSAY

With the plan for the essay laid out before you, you'll be clear about what you're trying to build before you even pick up your first 'brick'. Just like a building, your essay must be structurally sound.

Firstly, it will need an introduction. This is where you state your position on the issue and say explicitly what your essay intends to do and how it will do it. The introduction should present the main thrust of your approach in the first paragraph.

Next, develop your points in a logical order to make up the body of the essay. Try to connect them together so that the argument 'flows' along, and progresses one step at a time. Support your argument with evidence from your reading. It's not enough to speculate or theorise at university—you need to back up what you're saying with hard academic facts. You can do this by using examples and referring to published academic research on the subject you're discussing. At a first-year level, you're not expected to submit original research; you're simply being asked to prove that you understand a subject, have looked into it thoroughly and have provided your own analysis based on the available information.

When you've discussed your final point, lead your argument to a logical conclusion. Avoid introducing new information or ideas at the end of your essay: the conclusion must draw together your argument and finish your essay off cleanly. Keep it brief, and try to finish with a crisp, confident sentence that summarises your findings.

This is the basic framework for an effective essay. But the construction process is not over yet.

WHAT ARE FOOTNOTES?

Footnotes are like the doors and windows of your building. They let your reader in to look around your construction.

When you refer to academic research in your writing, it's essential to acknowledge the source of your information. This is true whether you actually quote from the material (lifting the exact words from the article or book, enclosed by quotation marks) or whether you include someone else's ideas, which you've incorporated into your essay in your own words.

It's not only perfectly acceptable to borrow from other people's ideas, it's expected. *But*, if you don't use footnotes, you're claiming that all the ideas in your essay are strictly your own work. If you don't acknowledge whose ideas and/or words you're drawing from, you're committing plagiarism. In effect, this means you're stealing someone else's work and passing it off as your own. Whether you mean to do this or not doesn't matter: *plagiarism is very serious and can get you kicked out of university*. So get into the habit of footnoting your work right from the start. You must do this every single time you include another person's ideas in your essays.

So what do footnotes look like? They're superscript (higher than the main line of type) numbers which you insert between the sentences of your essay. If you're using a word processing program, you can use the 'insert footnote' function, which will format the footnotes for you. You can choose to place your footnotes at the bottom of every page, or at the very end of the essay. The numerals can recommence with every page (if references appear at the bottom of each page) or run through the whole essay.

Footnotes must contain the author's name, the details of the article or book you're referring to, the city it was published in, the date of publication and the relevant page numbers. This information must be presented consistently. There are conventions that govern each element of the footnote reference, so you must pay attention to the presentation rules.

Here's an example of what a footnote looks like in the body of your essay.[1] Now check the bottom of this page, where you'll find a sample reference. Notice the punctuation, the use of italics for the title of the text and other formatting details. If you refer to the same author again later in the essay, you don't need to include the full quotation twice. A shortened version is more appropriate. Here's another example.[2] (Check the bottom of this page.) If another work by the same author is cited in the same group of footnotes, a short title should be added.[3] (Check the bottom of this page again.)

The examples given are common stylistic approaches to footnoting, but there are a couple of different referencing styles to choose from. Ask your tutors which style particular departments prefer.

THE BIBLIOGRAPHY: THE FINISHING TOUCH

OK, you've added doors and windows to your essay construction. Now it's time to apply the plaster and paint to your sturdy new building. The bibliography finishes off the construction process and ensures that the essay is complete.

The general idea of a bibliography is to provide very specific information about the texts you've consulted. Like footnotes, bibliographies come in a range of styles, and once again it's a good idea to check with your tutors about the conventions they'd prefer you to use. In the meantime, here's a guide to the kind of information that should go into a bibliography.

To add a **book** you've used in your essay to your bibliography, you could do this (take note of the order of elements and the correct punctuation to use):

---

1. Elizabeth Hardy, *University for Beginners: The Mysteries Revealed*, Sydney: New Holland, 2002, p. 42.
2. Hardy 2002, p. 42.
3. Hardy, *Doctorates for Beginners*, 2000, p.7.

Hardy, Elizabeth. *University for Beginners: The Mysteries Revealed.* Sydney, New Holland, 2002.

A **journal article** requires a bit more detail, and could look like this (again, pay attention to details like order of the elements, italics and punctuation):

Malouf, David. 'A first place: The mapping of a world', *Southerly*, vol. 45, 1985, pp.3–10.

Internet sites are different again. There are many schools of thought on this one, but in general, you need to provide all the information necessary for the person reading your essay to be able to find that particular site again. This will include the title of the page (if there is one), name of the author, the address of the site (or the URL), date of publication on the web (if known), and the date you accessed it. For example:

Michelangelo and the Value of Art, David Banach, http://www.anselm. edu/homepage/dbanach/mol.htm, 3 May 2002.

Whichever style of bibliography you adopt, be consistent, and don't swing back and forth between different styles. Inconsistent referencing makes you look like you've thrown the essay together and don't care about the details. As always, tutors notice this kind of thing.

A few other points to note include:
- The author's surname comes in front of his/her first name, unlike in a footnote where the surname comes second.
- The order of entries is alphabetical, based on the authors' surnames.
- The use of capitals in a book title is best kept to a minimum.

ESSAY-WRITING STYLE: EIGHT KEY POINTS

There are several golden rules of essay writing at a university level. Let's go through the most important ones.

1. Remember that an essay is a formal, assessable piece of work. Your final grade for the unit will be partly determined by each of your essays. Consequently, you should treat this as a serious piece of writing. Eliminate all slang, casual language, and anything else which makes your essay look like a note you've scribbled to a mate. Don't try to be funny or offhand; this creates a clear impression that you're not taking the task seriously, and you'll be marked accordingly.

2. Write clearly and correctly. Every single sentence should make sense and have a point to it. Start each new paragraph with a topic sentence that provides a coherent introduction to each set of new ideas.

3. The best essays are the product of more than one draft. Don't expect to write a flawless final copy the first time you sit down to begin your essay. Simply get your ideas down in a logical order to start with, and be prepared to rewrite and edit, polishing up any parts that are a bit garbled or need clarification.

4. NEVER hand in your essay without proofreading it first. This involves reading it through silently and slowly in your head, looking closely for typos or spelling mistakes, and missing punctuation. Then read it through again, this time out loud to yourself. Hopefully, you'll be able to *hear* which sentences don't quite make sense or are missing a word. Break up any sentences which ramble on and on, and make them into two or more smaller, clearer statements. Proofreading guarantees you will produce a tighter, higher-quality piece of work.

5. If you possibly can, word-process your work. This makes it much easier for your tutor to read, and also enables you to refine two or three drafts of your essay without having to write the whole thing out again. *Run the spell-check function through your essay before*

you print it out for proofreading. This will take only a minute or two and you'll be surprised at what you may have missed with the naked eye. Make sure you have either one backup copy of your computer file and/or a photocopy of your work. Very occasionally, essays can get lost after you've submitted them, so unless you're happy to start your essay again from scratch, make a copy of your work before you hand it in.

6. Stick to the set word limit. Your tutor will be horrified rather than impressed if you turn in 3000 words (or 500 words!) when you've been asked to write 1500. Keeping within these set parameters is part of the discipline of writing an essay, and your ability to do this will certainly have a bearing on your mark.

7. Avoid using the first person, as in 'I think this was an interesting idea', or 'I believe Wordsworth was a good poet'. Remember, you're supposed to be *analysing* an issue based on the available research, not just giving your opinion. You can say, 'Based on so-and-so's research it would seem that ...' or 'Current work in this field indicates ...'—anything that indicates you've consulted the authorities. The essay is not asking you what you *think*, it's asking you to follow the rules of the essay genre. This always means that analysis is required.

8. Don't make one of the most common mistakes in essay writing: retelling the relevant story rather than answering the essay question. For example, if you're supposed to be discussing an event in history, don't just recap what happened and who did what when. Your tutor already knows these details—that's why he or she is teaching it. Keep the question in the front of your mind and think about how you're going to answer it using information about the historical event. *Analyse, don't summarise.*

FIVE GOOD REASONS TO MASTER ESSAY WRITING

When you get your essay back, naturally you'll be most interested in getting a look at the final mark written there in bold red pen. But, whether the red number triggers joy or despair, there's a lot more to an essay than the grade itself. Here are five good reasons for bothering to learn the dreaded art of essay writing.

1. Essays show you how to improve.

Take a look at those comments written in the margins and scattered here and there throughout the essay. These are like little neon lights: there you have, in writing, a list of your strengths and weaknesses. Did you get a few extra ticks for a certain paragraph? Go back and reread it and work out why, then do more of that kind of thing in future. Did you submit an essay filled with bad grammar and spelling mistakes? Don't commit the same crime twice—it's not hard to spend a few minutes cleaning these up before you hand in your work. Learn to accept constructive criticism graciously. OK, it may temporarily dent your ego, but it can also be a road map that gives you clear directions to getting better marks.

2. Essays are dress rehearsals for exams.

Many exams require you to write a number of essays. If you learn effective essay-writing techniques during the semester, you'll be familiar with the requirements of the form by the time exams roll around. This can be a big plus when you're under some serious time pressure in an exam situation. You'll be a lot more relaxed if you already know what you're doing.

3. Essays can lift your semester grade.

Usually, essays are part of a unit's ongoing assessment. If you can learn from your mistakes and continue to improve, you'll find that you're probably going into the final exam from a position of strength. Say, for example, that your exam is worth 20 per cent of your final grade. You can shore up the other 80 per cent of available marks during the semester when you have time to refine and polish the work you submit as essays. In some courses, essays comprise between 75 and 100 per cent of the total assessment.

4. Essays teach you written communication skills.
When you plan an essay and then write a piece of work which has a structure, a logical argument and operates within set word limits, you're honing your ability to communicate in writing. If your writing itself is also clear and elegant, and your argument coherent and measured, you have a skill that's in demand by probably 99 per cent of employers. This kind of disciplined training can give you the confidence to write in a variety of forms and situations, both personally and professionally, for the rest of your life.

5. Essays force you to organise your thoughts.
By the time you finish an essay you will have discussed a topic you may have known nothing at all about a few weeks previously. You've gathered information and sorted through it so that it makes sense and supports your position on the issue in question. You've learned to think in a structured, logical and reasonable way. This is a problem-solving skill which will come in handy again and again, long after the gates of academia have banged shut behind you.

5. HOW TO PASS EXAMS

Exams. No word can strike more fear into the heart of the new student. You may be terrified that you'll fall to pieces as soon as you turn over the exam paper, or go completely blank when faced with questions about topics you in fact know really well. Or maybe you're concerned you won't be sufficiently prepared come exam time.

Follow the three-point strategy below and you'll find yourself getting through even the toughest exam.

STEP 1: PREPARE FOR BATTLE

It sounds too obvious for words, but for many people, this is a major stumbling block. They are simply not prepared to go into an exam fighting. So what does preparing for battle entail?

First off, it's essential to find out the latest, correct information about the exam dates, venues and times. Check the noticeboards on campus and take down all the relevant information. Write these details in three or four places: your diary, your wall calendar, your monthly planner. Make sure you're aware, in advance, of where you're supposed to be, when, and for which exam. If you wake up late the morning of your first exam and can't remember where it's being held, you'll have entered a waking nightmare. By the time you *do* find the exam room, you'll be so stressed it'll take a superhuman effort to be able to concentrate enough to even spell your name right.

You'd be surprised how many people get their exam times and dates wrong. *Don't* rely on your mates to give you the right details. Find out yourself.

So, make a plan for getting to the right exam, at the right venue, on the right day. Have several pens, pencils and any specialist equipment you need set out and ready to go.

Once you know your exam timetable, it's essential to make a strategy which allocates your available study time in appropriate chunks. Work out how many hours you can devote to each exam, taking into account that you may have to do extra work on the harder units, or the exam that carries more marks for your overall semester grade. Write your plan down, mapping out a timetable of study for each subject.

When you've decided how many hours you'll spend on each unit, sit down with the material you must revise and refine your plan, allocating time to different sections within each unit. Bear in mind that you probably won't be expected to regurgitate every last detail from a semester's worth of lectures, so focus on the topics most likely to be in the final exam. You can make educated guesses as to what's likely to be in the exam from picking up hints dropped in tutes and lectures, and by photocopying exam papers from previous years. These will be in the library and are well worth a look.

Exam preparation really puts your filing system and note-taking techniques to the test. Generally speaking, it's way too late to try and learn new material very close to exams. This is a time for revision, not for trying to cram a semester's worth of new information into your brain. So read through your existing notes, summarise them and condense them further. Make sure you understand the key points of the issues you think will probably be in the exams. Draw up some practice essay plans and think about the points you'd like to cover in the exam if you're asked a question on a particular topic.

By preparing yourself this thoroughly, you maximise your chances of walking into the exam feeling confident and prepared.

STEP 2: FINE-TUNE YOUR ATTITUDE

Your state of mind as you go into an exam is all-important. Exams are by nature mysterious, and you can never fully predict exactly what you'll be faced with when you turn the paper over. But remember, everyone's in the same boat, and all you can do is confront the exam battlefield with confidence. Remind yourself that you've prepared as well as possible, and that you're ready for battle.

Be aware that outside the exam room will be little groups of panic merchants all promising each other that they're ill prepared and bound to fail. Don't join any of these groups—their negativity is contagious. Stand off to one side and tell yourself that you're ready to ace the exam. Mentally run through the main points of the key issues. Glance through your notes and reassure yourself that you know what you're talking about. Take some deep breaths and remain calm.

Once you're in the exam room, continue to remind yourself that you're ready and well prepared. Your attitude before you turn over the exam paper can determine how well you perform in the next couple of hours. If you think to yourself, 'OK, bring it on, let's write a brilliant exam,' then you'll be thinking clearly and confidently and will be much more likely to create a positive result.

Your state of mind is your choice. Make a decision about how you want to perform before you walk into the exam room, and turn over the paper.

STEP 3: LET THE BATTLE BEGIN

In addition to choosing a calm and positive mental state, you have several other secret weapons you can put to good use once the action has begun on the exam battlefield.

The first is to listen to the supervisor's instructions. Pay attention to what is said at the beginning of the exam. The supervisor will talk about the amount of time you have to complete the exam, and also let you know what kinds of materials are allowable: reference books, calculators, and so on.

Many exams include a ten-minute reading period in which you can make notes on your answer booklet. Find out if this is the case in each of your exams by listening to the supervisor and reading the instructions on the front of the exam paper. These ten minutes are your ace in the hole. Here's what you should aim to achieve in this vital period of time:

- Read the instructions on the exam paper. Are any questions compulsory? How many do you have to answer from each section? Turn the paper over—there may be more questions to choose from on the back. Make sure you understand exactly what's required of you before you even look at the questions themselves.

- Read the actual questions calmly and thoroughly. Decide quickly but carefully which ones you'll answer and note down the numbers of the questions on your answer booklet. Make your decisions logically and confidently. You won't have time to change your mind once the exam begins.

- Work out how much time you should devote to each question. Take into account how many marks each question is worth, and spend more time crafting the answers that represent more marks.

- Map out a quick answer plan for each of your questions. This is so important that it's worth doing even if you spend a couple more minutes on it after the writing period officially starts. In your answer plan, jot down all the points you can remember about the topic, and sketch out a rough structure for your argument. This plan will keep you on track when you start to write. Remember, you can't rewrite or edit very much in an exam; it can really throw you if you get to the end of an answer and only then remember the key point which should have been slotted in right at the beginning.

Once you've read the paper, chosen the questions you are going to answer, allocated appropriate lengths of time to each question and mapped out an answer plan to each one, your ten minutes will most likely be up and the time to start writing will have begun. Here are some points to keep in mind once the exam begins in earnest.

- Keep track of your timing. If you're coming to the end of the time you've allocated to your first question, force yourself to wind up your answer. If you have more information you'd have liked to include, but have run out of time to write another five paragraphs, note down your other ideas in point form. This lets the marker know that you've got more to say but no more time to say it in. Remember, there's really no point in writing the perfect answer to one question and running out of time for the other three questions. You can only be marked on what you write. So write *something* for each question you're required to answer.

- Try to write legibly. While obviously you won't be marked on your handwriting, your marker will probably be irritated at having to decode little spidery scribblings or big messy scrawls. You also create an impression of being calm and well prepared if you write answers which don't look like they were written in a state of intense panic. Do your best to pay attention to spelling and grammar, too—remember, these things convey an idea as to whether you're floundering out of your depth or whether you're confident and in control of your material.

- If there's a question you know you can answer really well, tackle that first. Beginning with material you know thoroughly can really boost your confidence. This relaxes you and you'll feel more self-assured when you begin your next answer.

Remember, the exam room doesn't have to be a torture chamber. Exams are written to test you on your understanding of work you've already done. They're not designed to deliberately trick you into failing. Follow the above strategies and prepare to emerge triumphant from the exam battleground.

HOW TO FAIL ANY EXAM: THE TEN BIGGEST MISTAKES YOU CAN MAKE

Here's a detailed guide to what NOT to do when preparing for and sitting exams. These non-productive behaviours can be avoided, especially once you know what to look out for. Remember, exams are not as scary as many people think. You can maximise your chances of success in your next exam by not doing any of the following:

1. DON'T leave your preparation to the last minute so that you are frantically trying to learn new material the night before the exam.

2. DON'T make your notes difficult to find and read. You can't afford to spend most of your preparation period trying to track down a semester's worth of work and then trying to make sense of cryptic or illegible scrawls.

3. DON'T mistake the pre-exam study break for a holiday and spend much of the time catching up with friends and having late nights out. If you do, you run the risk of getting run down and falling sick just before the exam.

4. Even worse, DON'T turn up to the exam with a hangover and only three hours of sleep.

5. DON'T hang out with the people who are convinced they're going to fail before they've even sat the exam. Their fear will rub off on you, and so will their defeatist attitude.

6. DON'T shift into panic mode the minute you enter the exam room. Plan your answers, allocate your time and listen calmly to instructions.

7. DON'T forget to turn through all the pages of the exam paper before you begin writing, otherwise you may discover there are another ten questions to answer in the last three minutes of the exam.

8. DON'T use slang or swear words in your answer. (Believe it or not, this happens.) This approach may help you to let off steam if the exam is harder than you anticipated, but it's guaranteed to earn you very, very low marks—and maybe an appointment with the Dean.

9. DON'T leave the exam an hour early, or turn up late. Use every minute of writing time you have. If you finish early, expand your answers.

10. DON'T try to cheat. If you're caught, you're likely to be kicked out of university.

PART TWO: STUDENT SURVIVAL SKILLS

6. TRIUMPHING OVER STRESS

By about halfway through the first semester you'll have handed in several pieces of assessment and have a pretty good idea as to how the whole system works. You're probably finding that Planet University is not as completely alien as you'd initially thought. Nevertheless, the relentless deadlines and ongoing workload that are a way of life in this environment might be making you feel a bit overwhelmed.

If so, it may be time to spend a few minutes on stress management.

TELLTALE SIGNS OF STRESS

It's easy for stress to creep up on you. Before you know it you're feeling cranky or tired a lot of the time. Perhaps you're having trouble sleeping, or picking up every flu bug around. Worrying about money or having dramas with housemates are also commonplace.

Let's face it, starting university is a major life change for most people, so some stress is probably inevitable. But it doesn't have to be the main feature of your university experience.

TAKE ACTION—QUICK!

Think about your lifestyle and how balanced it is. Are you studying and working too much and feeling resentful that you don't have time for a social life? Or maybe the reverse is true for you—you've spent so much time in the swirling currents of university social life that now you're terrified that you won't pass your units. If either of these descriptions fits, you need to take steps to get some balance back into your life.

Start by creating a picture of your average week. Write down the names of the days of the week, and under each day note down your normal activities for that day in a typical week. Include weekends, and list *all* your activities: lectures, tutes, study time, social time, hours spent at a part-time job, afternoons at the pub or coffee shop—everything. When you've done this for each day you'll have in front of you a detailed picture of an average week in your life right now. It should be clear what you need to change to even out the current imbalance and reduce your stress levels.

Try rescheduling your time. On a clean piece of paper, list the activities you will do *from now on* from week to week. Depending on whether you're spending too much or too little time studying, you may want to swap a study session for a movie, or exchange a morning in the coffee shop for a morning in the library. Make the necessary changes now, so that neither your health nor your marks suffer.

TEN QUICK STRESS BUSTERS

What if it's not your weekly routine that's the problem but you're still experiencing a general reduction of interest in study and a lowering of energy levels? You're probably not taking the time to recognise your progress so far. Try some of these ways of rekindling your sense of enthusiasm for university:

1. Reward yourself. Did you get a better mark than you expected for an essay? Did you make it to more tutes than you thought you would? Buy yourself something to mark the achievement. It doesn't have to be expensive—a block of decadent chocolate, a few beers. Anything that makes you feel good and functions as a symbolic reward.

2. Have a chat with someone you haven't made contact with for ages. Catching up with friends—especially if you feel that university has taken over your life—can be really uplifting. Chances are you'll have a laugh and regain some perspective. A phone call and half an hour of your time cost almost nothing.

3. Remember to exercise. When you have a really busy schedule, often exercise is the first part of your routine to be sacrificed. You may be feeling sluggish and low in enthusiasm because your body is demanding to be exercised. If your mind is the only part of you getting a work-out, take a swim or go for a walk in the fresh air. You'll notice that you feel considerably more positive and energetic.

4. Breathe deeply. If you're worried about assignments or exams, both your mind and body will be tense rather than relaxed. Get on top of your feelings of anxiety by taking a few deep breaths and stretching your body gently. Concentrate on moving the oxygen through your system, and focus on releasing the sources of your stress each time you exhale.

5. Take some time to rediscover the things you enjoy. What did you do to relax before your life became dominated by university? You won't feel so resentful of your study commitments if you make time to incorporate into your daily routine the hobby or pastime you once loved.

6. Try a change of scene. If you're sick of looking at the same old walls, try studying in a more inspiring setting. If you always walk the same route to work or lectures, go another way next time. Meet friends for coffee in a place none of you have ever been to before. The smallest of changes can shake up your routine and refresh you.

7. Take regular breaks from study. If you force yourself to study for hours on end without stopping to rest, you're simply pushing too hard. It's very difficult to concentrate for long periods of time without a break, so you're probably not making as much progress with your work as you may think. Drag yourself away from that keyboard: go for a walk, make a phone call or put the kettle on. You'll be more focused and positive when you sit down to work again.

8. Maintain your enthusiasm for university by documenting your progress to date. Think about how much you know now compared to your first day on campus. Make a list of what you've achieved—you may be surprised to discover how far you've already come.

9. Get proper rest. Take stock of your bedroom and make any necessary changes to improve the quality of your sleep. Do you need heavier curtains so you don't wake up as the sun rises? Do you need to replace your loudly ticking clock with a silent one? Make a conscious effort not to eat a heavy meal late at night—your body may be too busy furiously digesting to relax fully into sleep. And what about coffee and soft drinks: are you drinking too much caffeine late in the afternoon or evening? Making one or two tiny changes like this can really improve your quality of sleep and stop you feeling permanently tired.

10. If your workload and budget permit, think about taking a couple of days off from study completely. So long as you have no assignments due and are not behind in your work, have a mini-holiday and make a commitment to relaxing and unwinding rather than worrying. This can really put your problems in perspective.

Remember, it's quite simply unrealistic to expect that you'll never be stressed while you're at university. You're in a formidable new environment that throws challenges at you one after the other. This is bound to produce moments of anxiety and apprehension. Recognise that this is perfectly normal, and then try some of the above stress remedies to get yourself back on an even keel.

However, if you find that you seem to be *always* stressed and worried, it's worth checking out what kind of help is available to you on campus. You may be able to take a stress-reduction course, or make an appointment with a counsellor who can talk through your problems with you. Don't hesitate to call Student Services and find out what kind of support you can access. It's impossible to enjoy university if you're feeling stretched to breaking point.

DO IT NOW! THREE WAYS OF BEATING PROCRASTINATION

Putting things off is the easiest thing in the world to do. When you've got an essay to start or tute preparation to do, it's truly amazing how many other things can suddenly seem vitally important: you *must* catch that movie while it's still showing, or make four or five of those essential phone calls … Incredibly enough, when you're in deep procrastination mode even housework seems imperative!

If any of these scenes ring a bell with you, you're on intimate terms with the procrastination monster. But this monster can be dealt with, despite its power to distract you. So throw down that vacuum cleaner and try one of these approaches:

1. Make a date, a definite commitment, to start that task you've been dreading. Write the date of the commitment down somewhere prominent: on the fridge, in your diary, on your calendar. Schedule your life around the task and make it the central activity of your day or week. If someone calls and asks you out for a beer or a shopping frenzy, organise to meet with them another day. Don't let someone else give you an excuse to break the commitment.

2. If scheduling a starting date doesn't work for you, then the direct approach may be your best bet. Don't give yourself time to double-book your day or fill it with more fun things to do. Open that textbook and start reading, or turn on your computer and start writing—NOW!

3. If you think the task you're putting off will be boring or difficult, commit to doing it for just half an hour. Set up a clock on your desk and stick to that time limit. If the task is something you really loathe doing, try chipping away at it in short bursts rather than spending an entire day on it. You're much more likely to be able to tolerate a little bit at a time. Then all you need to do is put in enough of these little blocks of time to get the task finished.

7. STAYING MOTIVATED IS UP TO YOU

For many people, getting into university was the easy part; it's staying there that's hard.

One of the biggest challenges involved in getting a degree lies in the fact that you have to motivate yourself to study. While most of your tutors would prefer to give you decent grades if they could, if the level of your work isn't up to scratch, well, basically it's your problem, not theirs.

So what can you do if you find you're falling behind with your work and finding it difficult to imagine yourself seeing the semester through? Here are some self-motivating ideas for staying on track.

HOW DO YOU SEE CHALLENGES?

Many people really come into their own when faced with a difficult task. Try thinking of getting your degree as the ultimate personal test—and one that you're determined to pass with flying colours. This is the mind-set of the true university survivor. You may have heard of the motivation strategy used by many high-pressure corporations, whereby the company's top executives are dropped off in the bush for a week. Left to their own devices, and with only the bare minimum of equipment and provisions, these employees are forced to rely on their own ingenuity to survive. In just the same way, you're facing a challenge that may sometimes be harder than you expected.

Not every aspect of university life is fun, it's true. But, like the executives who survived a week in the bush, you too can stagger triumphantly to the end of your degree—still alive, stronger, wiser and with a valuable qualification gripped tightly in your hand.

DON'T BE OVERWHELMED BY HOW MUCH YOU HAVE TO DO

What if the image of yourself on graduation night seems too far off to work as an effective motivator? The moment of victory may seem too distant— a whole lifetime away. If this is the case, try focusing on one goal at a time instead. Break your semester into smaller, less daunting units. It's still a good idea to plan out your whole semester's assessment and write down the submission dates for each assignment. But once you've got a handle on how the big picture looks, try shifting your focus back to a smaller scale. Move through each assignment in turn, and make it to the end of semester one step at a time.

TRACKING YOUR PROGRESS

If you're despairing about how much further you still have to go down the degree road, stop and think about how far you've already come. Take a few minutes to write down a 'then' and 'now' list. What were you worried about before you came to university? What progress have you made with a particular problem? Does it seem like a childish fear now? Tape up a list of your triumphs in your study area so you'll be reminded of how much you've already achieved on a daily basis. This can be really encouraging, and spur you on to further success.

A MENTOR OR ROLE MODEL CAN HELP

When you're struggling to stay motivated, it can really help to hook up with a more experienced person who's already been in your shoes. Check to see whether your university runs a mentoring program. If it doesn't, you may be able to independently link up with another student who is further along the road and willing to offer some guidance to a new student. Alternatively, your mentor could be someone who's already working in the field you want to enter, or you could come to an arrangement with an inspiring relative or family friend who has always taken an interest in you.

When you've chosen a person you think could be a reliable source of support and inspiration, you should approach that person and ask if he or she would be willing to act as your mentor. If the person agrees (and most people will be flattered and delighted that you think of them as a role model), sit down together and work out some 'rules', covering issues such as how often you'll meet and what you'll require of each other. Although you should stay in regular contact with your mentor, make sure you don't overstep the boundaries you've just mapped out. Don't call your mentor three times a day or late at night, for example, or demand an urgent meeting when he or she is having a particularly busy week.

You can also benefit from other people's experience by reading biographies of figures you admire. You may be surprised at the obstacles most people have had to overcome before reaching their goals. It can be really uplifting to realise that everyone has had to deal with challenges and problems in their lives. Even the most successful people—those who seem to achieve effortlessly—have had to struggle with self-doubt and lack of motivation at some time.

CLARIFY WHAT YOU WANT OUT OF UNIVERSITY

Remind yourself about what attracted to you to university in the first place. Make a list if it helps. Were you sick of slaving away in a dead-end job where you weren't appreciated? Were you interested in learning more about a certain subject, or determined to get a particular qualification?

Then spend some time thinking about why you're at university now. Is the reason you wanted to go initially still relevant? University might have already turned out to be very different from your original expectations. Make an amended list of why you should continue to give tertiary education a chance.

You must have had at least one good reason to want to spend time on Planet University initially, and you can probably think of many more reasons now to stay. Remind yourself of those reasons whenever you're feeling sick of the whole process and lacking in motivation.

FOUR PROVEN METHODS FOR TAKING CONTROL OF YOUR TIME

Your level of self-motivation is directly affected by how well you manage your time. It's hard to stay motivated if you always feel rushed and pressured; it then becomes tempting to throw in the towel and do something less stressful. If you're finding it difficult to juggle the different elements of your life, perhaps you need to examine your time-management skills. Try some of these techniques for escaping the time-poverty trap.

1. Learn to say 'no'.

Believe it or not, this is one of the most effective ways in the world of taking back control of your time. Think about how often you agree to do things when you don't really want to. Do you say 'yes' to every demand on your time because you don't want to upset people by refusing their requests?

If this is ringing some bells, it may be time to start saying 'no' to the things you'd rather not do. Be warned: the first couple of times, it's pretty difficult. Complying with everyone else's needs or entreaties is a habit and it can be tough to break. But you can do it with a bit of practice. Rather than saying 'yes' automatically when someone asks you for a favour, try hesitating for a few seconds. You don't have to be rude—you can simply say, 'Sorry, I'm not available then', or 'Sorry, I have other plans.'

Try it. Once you break the 'yes' habit, you'll be amazed at how great it feels to have control of your time again.

2. Get a diary and start scheduling!

It's hard to get a handle on your time if you don't know *where* you're supposed to be, or *when*. At the moment, you might associate diaries with high-powered executives. But in fact, diaries are a practical, useful tool that almost everyone can benefit from using.

You don't have to get a huge diary—or an ugly one. Pick one that you really like, full of quotes, artwork, or jokes and cartoons that will make you laugh. You're much more likely to use this valuable tool often if you find it attractive and appealing.

It's also a good idea to get a diary that's small enough to carry around with you. That way, you can note down appointments and new commitments as they pop up during the day. Your diary becomes a record of your deadlines and a testament to your progress. It's very satisfying to be able to tick off everything on today's list of things to do. Where better to keep such a list than in your diary?

3. Use 'dead' time effectively.

Think about all the things you do in the course of a day that don't require 100 per cent concentration. Could you be using this 'dead' time more effectively? Instead of just zoning out while you do the dishes, could you recite your French verbs or chemistry formulae aloud to yourself? Can you mentally run through a tute presentation while you vacuum the living room? How about using the time you spend in the shower to remind yourself of your goals and motivation for being at university? Listen to a tape of a lecture while you're cooking dinner. Read an extra chapter of your textbook while waiting for the bus. Using this kind of time productively will help you to get more done in less time.

4. Minimise distractions.

Think for a minute about how many demands are placed on your time during any given day. Fitting in enough time for reading, getting to lectures, preparing for tutorials, travelling to and from university and studying at home is enough of a challenge. Add to that mix a part-time job, a relationship, a social life and family obligations and you have an unlimited number of potential distractions!

If you're feeling under pressure or have a deadline looming, now is the time to become aware of who or what distracts you from your studies, and make the necessary changes. If you have a lonely neighbour who rushes over to see you the second you get back from university, you'll have to explain that you can't have a cup of tea with him this week. If the phone is constantly ringing while you're trying to get an essay finished, buy an answering machine and get back to your callers when it's convenient for you. Or just take the phone off the hook for an hour or two to get some peace. If someone is at the front door hoping to sell you a subscription or a new religion, simply say 'no thank you'.

You shouldn't feel guilty about making your progress at university a priority. How you spend your time is your business, and no-one else can earn this degree for you. Your lonely neighbour or the charity door-knocker are probably not going to write your essay for you!

8. FROM CATERPILLAR TO SOCIAL BUTTERFLY

So far, we've looked at how to handle some of the personal and academic challenges you'll face at university. But there's more to getting a degree than locking yourself away with your books and emerging at the end of three or more years with a framed diploma. Think about it: if you don't meet people now, who are you going to drink champagne with on graduation night?

As well as being a stimulating learning environment, university also represents a unique social nexus. You may never again find yourself surrounded by such a huge range of intelligent people. And you're being thrown together every week in lectures and tutorials because you have some common interests. This is a truly amazing opportunity.

Many people strike up really valuable friendships at university. You'll probably make some lifelong friends here. You could end up having a long-term relationship with someone sitting in your next lecture—you might even marry someone in your tute group! Moreover, leads to jobs often come up through university contacts. And if all these prospects don't convince you of the importance of having an active social life at university, remember that it can be pretty lonely having no-one to talk to at lunch time or while waiting for lectures to start. Potential friends are all around you: all you have to do is meet them.

HOW TO MEET YOUR NEW FRIENDS

So how *do* you go about forming these exciting new alliances? If you've come to university straight from school, you may have a small crew of people you already know from there who have started at the same university as you. These people can be a great source of comfort and support for you in your first few weeks. But don't limit yourself to hanging out only with people you already know. Make a conscious decision to expand your circle of friends, and start doing so as soon as possible. If you wait too long, it's harder to break into the little groups which inevitably start to form.

If you're a mature-age student, you might not know a soul in any of your courses. This is not as terrifying as it sounds; there are many sources of support waiting for you. Many universities run mature-age social groups and can guide you towards a range of helpful services, including childcare.

Stay alert to friend-making opportunities: scope out your tutes for compatible company; start chatting to the people who look interesting or friendly outside lectures; take the initiative and ask someone to have a coffee with you. You're guaranteed to have something in common with your fellow students. Talk about the last lecture, the course in general, your experience of university so far, and how you got there. Don't be afraid of picking the 'wrong' person to talk to. You don't have to sign a contract to be friends for life—you're simply checking out the other people in your course and seeing who might be interesting.

Once you've done this a few times, you'll have people to talk to before and after classes, and discuss assignment questions with. Soon you'll probably be making plans for the weekend with your new mates as well. Before you know it, a whole support network will have been formed by your friendly actions.

MORE FRIENDLY PLACES TO VISIT

As you get around the campus, it's an idea to keep a regular eye on the noticeboards. This is where you'll see posters about social clubs, meetings and a wide range of other social events. Film nights, wine and cheese evenings, guest speakers on weird and wonderful topics—all these are prime opportunities to make easy, relaxed contact with other interesting people.

It can be difficult to pluck up the courage to turn up to these events by yourself, so try rustling up some support for the evening. Either ask someone you already know, or invite one of your potential new mates in the coffee shop after a lecture. Even better, get a group going and you'll have created another opportunity to get to know even more new people.

The university bar is also an easy place to get talking to potential new friends. Often there are bands booked to play, and this makes for a laid-back, sociable atmosphere where you can meet people who are probably there for the same reason you are. The bar is also a useful place to get to know students who are taking courses in other faculties. Their university experiences may be entirely different from yours, and they'll be more than happy to talk to someone with another perspective. Chatting to people from other disciplines can show you a whole other side of Planet University that you may otherwise never see.

The key to thriving socially at university, then, is to connect with people as often as you can. Smile and start a conversation at every opportunity, and get out to the social events that interest you. Establish these new alliances sooner rather than later. Once you've made your first new friend, and attended your first couple of film nights, you'll be embarrassed that you ever hesitated to take the initiative.

A WORD FROM THE VOICE OF REASON

Making new friends and having an active social life is vital if you want to enjoy university and get the most out of the experience. *But*, make sure you don't let your social efforts take precedence over your academic ones. Don't end up failing units because you spent your study time at the bar making new friends.

The goal is to achieve a balance between work and play. With no-one to check on you every minute, it's up to you to determine your own limits. Make the right decisions now and you'll end up with a marketable degree, good friends and useful contacts for your future career. In some courses, failing units results in you being banned from continuing. If this happens, you'll either have to repeat the semester or year, or go and find a job—without the advantages of your university qualification. Think about it, and make a wise choice now.

FIVE EASY STEPS TO MAKING FRIENDS

Although you may feel at first that you're alone in a sea of strange faces, it's not as hard as you think to transform some of those strangers into good friends. There are several things you can do to facilitate the friend-making process.

1. Get into the habit of smiling at people as you walk around campus. Before long you'll start to recognise the faces that always smile back. Then it's the most natural thing in the world to strike up a conversation and find out who these people are. Smiling makes you look friendly and approachable.

2. Pay attention to your body language. When you're waiting outside lectures, don't stand off to one side with your head down and your arms folded. Turn your face towards your fellow students and look directly at them. This is an easy place to make eye contact and start chatting with someone about the lecture you're both about to sit through.

3. Ask your potential new friends questions about themselves. Don't bombard them with lots of information about your childhood or your personal problems from the first second you talk to them; it's polite to find out about the other person first. Most people love talking about themselves, and asking questions is a great way to show that you're interested in getting to know more about them.

4. Find something that you like about the person you're talking to and compliment them on it. If they're wearing a T-shirt with your favourite band on it, for example, talk about that. If they're wearing an unusual

piece of jewellery, comment on it. The other person will probably be flattered and pleased to make contact with someone who has compatible tastes and interests, and the social skills to prove it.

5. Don't forget to actually introduce yourself to the people you meet. Find out their names so that they don't remain vaguely friendly presences you smile at now and then when you bump into them on campus. If you've spent some time chatting and get on really well with a person, ask for his or her phone number or email address, or arrange to meet for a coffee. Follow up with a short, friendly phone call or email message in the next couple of days.

9. MAKING ENDS MEET

While you're a student, you're unlikely to be kicking back enjoying the good life. The round-the-world cruises and mountains of caviar are still a couple of years off. But it's pretty hard to concentrate on getting your degree when you don't have money for a sandwich and coffee, or if you're worrying about how to pay the rent. You'll tend to find that instant noodles and packet soup get very boring if you have them every night for dinner. But what are your alternatives? Is there a way to survive financially as well as academically on Planet University?

The answer is a firm *yes*.

Adopting a survivor mentality helps. Some weeks you will be eating lentils and rice a lot more often than you'd like, and your wardrobe may suddenly no longer represent the cutting edge of fashion. You may not always be able to buy two rounds in a row at the pub. But other weeks you might find you have a little more and can treat yourself in small ways. Overall, it's important to remember that you don't need to embrace this lifestyle of reduced income forever—just long enough for you to get that degree in your hand. If you just wanted a regular pay cheque, you wouldn't be at university in the first place, right?

You came to university for a reason, and it can really help to remind yourself of what that reason was when times are a bit lean. Here are some ways of making those budget dollars stretch a little further.

PROTECT WHAT YOU ALREADY HAVE

Even though you may be frustrated that you can't afford some of the things you want right now, you probably already have quite a lot of valued possessions. Take measures to look after the things you already own. Refocusing your attention on what you have rather than what's lacking in your life is always a positive move. On a practical level, too, keeping track of where your stuff is and making sure it's secure will save you money in the long run, when you don't have to replace all your possessions after they're stolen!

While you might automatically lock your back door as you leave your house, many people don't take similar precautions once they arrive on campus. It may surprise you to discover that university is not a secluded, protected little world free from crime. So you can save yourself a lot of stress—and money—if you protect what you already have while you're at university too. Laptops, calculators, jackets, bikes, bags, books, and even study notes routinely go missing from various locations around university. Don't leave anything lying around the campus if you want it to be there when you get back.

INVESTIGATING SOURCES OF FINANCIAL AID

Have a chat to your student union about the kinds of financial aid available to students. There may be a range of different funding sources right under your nose, including book subsidies, scholarships, computer loans, student discounts and emergency loans. Some of these opportunities are not widely advertised, so you won't know if you don't ask. The people at the student union are constantly answering questions about funding, so it's not even worth feeling embarrassed about talking money with them.

If you're receiving Austudy or any form of social security benefits, make it your business to find out about your rights. There are all kinds of reduced-fee services available to you. You may be entitled to a health-care card, for instance. This card, and your student card, can get you discounts on a range of items from movie tickets to train passes and prescription medicines. Get on the phone to Centrelink and find out if you're eligible. (See the appendix for useful contact details.)

There are a wide range of free or cheap services available to you right on campus, too. Find out if the university medical centre bulk bills (if so, you just show your Medicare card and don't have to pay anything for the visit). You can take care of your emotional health by seeing the on-campus counsellor, and find out about available accommodation at the student services office. There may be a student employment service available, where you can access free job boards which advertise part-time and casual positions. Usually these employers are specifically looking for a student to fill the position—so you're already at least partly qualified! You can probably get free career planning advice from the student services office too. If there's a hairdresser on campus, I'm willing to bet you can get a student discount there as well. And don't forget the student rates on offer at the university gym and the range of books—some discounted—which you'll find at the co-op bookshop. Resources are all around you—just keep your eyes open and make it your mission to be aware of what's available.

GETTING A PART-TIME JOB

Whether or not you qualify for Austudy or a social security benefit, sometimes you just need some regular cash coming in. It may be time to bite the bullet and trade some of your spare time for money. You can either get a regular part-time job or do the occasional one-off gig whenever you need to. The jobs board on campus offers many opportunities for both kinds of part-time work. Register with the campus employment service and check its boards regularly—you may be surprised by what you find there.

Of course, there are plenty of other avenues which can lead to part-time work as well. Campus noticeboards are often pasted with fliers advertising opportunities for student workers. It's also a good idea to mention to anyone and everyone that you talk to that you're looking for part-time or casual work. You might be chatting to someone you barely know outside a lecture theatre, who knows of an opening and passes it on to you. Or a friend of a friend may have just spoken to an employer looking to take on someone exactly like you. Mention your desire for a part-time job to family, friends, shop assistants and even lecturers and tutors if you're on good terms with them. There are opportunities everywhere.

The internet can also be a useful job-seeking resource. There are endless job sites you can search. Although many are American, there are also Australian-based sites, and depending on your research skills you may be able to find something through this channel. Ask your student services office for help in searching the net for jobs. If you've left your job to come to university, or have held down *any* kind of job in the past, you already have some marketable skills. Try approaching similar companies to the ones you've already worked for, or register with an employment agency which specialises in your area.

Bear in mind that many part-time jobs pitched at students will not be the most stimulating jobs in the world. There are a lot of menial, mind-numbing jobs out there which you may be horrified to find yourself applying for. But remember: this is a short-term money-earner, not a job meant for delivering satisfaction. And you never know, a part-time job which is boring and not-so-well paid may easily lead to something better. Just don't believe for a minute that you can't do better. You can, and will: remember, that's what you're at university for—to get that piece of paper which will do wonders for both your self-esteem and your job prospects.

THE PROS AND CONS OF JUGGLING WORK AND STUDY

You may have discovered that a part-time (or even full-time) job is simply essential to your financial survival. For other people, working may be an irritating distraction that produces little extra money and takes up more time than it's worth. Whether you need to work a little or a lot while you're at university, it doesn't hurt to be aware of the positive and negative aspects of combining work and study.

THE CASE FOR WORKING WHILE YOU STUDY

- Your time-management skills will improve out of sight, as you learn to keep many balls in the air at once.

- Experience in the real world looks fantastic on your CV. It shows initiative and drive, and will impress most employers.
- Your time in the workplace may help to put your studies in perspective and remind you that there are a range of different lifestyles out there. University is important, but it's not the only thing in life.
- If you have taken a menial job you don't particularly enjoy, it can motivate you to get on with your degree and complete the qualifications that may lead to a better job, with higher status and much improved pay.
- If your job isn't too taxing and you can forget about it as soon as you leave the workplace, you'll worry less about money and focus more on your studies.
- Your job could get your foot in the door for future opportunities at your current workplace, or could lead to contact with other potential employers in related areas.
- A greater disposable income will make it easier to reward yourself for your successes at university. Going out to dinner or buying a bottle of champagne suddenly become possible.
- A job that's related to your course can be beneficial to your studies. For example, if you're working with unpublished data, or with colleagues who have first-hand experience in areas you're still learning about. This kind of job effectively represents an additional learning environment.

THE CASE AGAINST WORKING WHILE YOU STUDY

- Strict scheduling of your time will be necessary. You'll have less flexibility, as there will be certain times of the day and week that will have to be spent at work.
- It's easy to become very tired if you're cramming too much into your days. This feeling of fatigue can creep up on you and adversely affect your health if it's not quickly checked.
- It may be difficult to negotiate flexible hours with your employer to allow for the extra study time necessary around exams and when assignments are due.

- Your workload may cause you to miss lectures and tutorials, and fall behind in your course.
- Your job may interfere with your ability to socialise very much with fellow students, making you more isolated on campus.
- If you have an above-average student job that is interesting and full of future opportunities, you may be tempted to drop the degree altogether and enter the workforce full-time.
- Working part-time will almost certainly affect any Austudy or social security payments you may already be receiving. Check with the relevant agency about how much you can earn before your payments are reduced.
- If you change your enrolment to part-time to accommodate your job, your degree will take longer to complete.

HOW TO SPEND LESS

As a student, you have a huge advantage in the shopping stakes. You're not stuck in an office from sun-up to sundown, five days a week. Chances are you only have to be on campus at certain times during the week. So use some of the time you've set aside for socialising to shop around for the things you need; it can be amazing how much money you can save if you bother to check a couple of different places for the items you're looking for. This way, you're investing time instead of money. (And, if you use the *Yellow Pages* rather than physically checking different shops, you can reduce your time investment as well.)

SAVING ON GROCERIES

The benefits of flexible hours extend to shopping for groceries. Get to the supermarket on Saturday afternoon, when some items (such as meat and some vegetables) are reduced to clear.

Before you hit the shops, make sure you have a list with you. Force yourself to stick to the list and you'll reduce the number of impulse buys you make. While chocolate or beer are a lot more fun than toilet paper, ask yourself—which is more essential? And if you have a snack before you head out, you'll also be less likely to deviate from your list. Shopping when you're hungry means you buy more impulse food, so eat first and pay less.

Experiment with cheaper versions of your preferred products. If you're reluctant to do this, think about whether you'd prefer to have perfect hair maintained by an expensive conditioner or whether you'd like regular meals while you finish your degree. Likewise, this is a good time to over-come any embarrassment about buying generic brand products. You can save a surprising amount of money this way.

Finally, keep your receipt so you can split the grocery bill with the other members of your household. This helps to make sure that everyone pays their fair share.

THE JOYS OF OP-SHOPPING

Opportunity shops offer one-stop shopping for an A to Z of student needs. You can pretty much find everything you need here, from dinner plates to T-shirts. The kitchen sections of many op-shops have very cheap cooking and eating utensils, and you can set yourself up here for next to nothing—and the money you do spend goes to charity.

Have a look around the bigger op-shops for office supplies, too. Often you can find second-hand lever-arch files and clipboards being thrown out for around 50 cents. Keeping both your eyes and your mind open can save you a fortune. Remember, one day you'll be able to splash out and buy what you want … but first you need to finish that degree!

STUDYING ON THE CHEAP

The price of some textbooks is enough to make you want to drop out of university before you even make it to your first class. It can be a terrifying prospect to have to scrape together hundreds and hundreds of dollars to buy several large textbooks. As always, there are alternatives.

Before you fork out your life savings for a library of books you proba-bly won't read cover-to-cover anyway, it's wise to get some advice. The course controller of the unit which demands these books can advise you on which ones are essential. Sometimes you only need one of the books at the beginning of the course, and you can save up for others as the semester progresses.

Another avenue to explore is the library. Most often, the essential textbooks are placed in the Closed Reserve section (see Chapter 3 for more about how the library works). This part of the library provides ongoing access to the important texts and you can photocopy or take notes on the chapters you are required to read—all without buying the book.

If you have a friend doing the same course, you can discuss splitting the cost of the more expensive books and then sharing them between you. This can be a bit of a challenge, though, when assignments and exams approach and you have to fight to get access to the books. Only try this if you can come to a firm and fair agreement about who gets the books on which days. This is easier, of course, if you share a house, but it can still cause problems if you both want to read Chapter 5 on the same night.

The second-hand bookshop on campus may also hold copies of the books you need, at greatly reduced prices. But make sure you check on the edition required for your course. Often reading lists are updated from year to year, and it's pretty frustrating to spend $70 on an outdated version of the book you really needed. It's a good idea to check the second-hand bookshop as soon as you get your reading lists, as the books you'll find there tend to sell out quickly, particularly at the beginning of a new semester.

Your local and state libraries are also potential sources of free access to books. They're unlikely to hold any technical or specialist textbooks, but if you're after something in the literary line, or some general background reading, you may come across some treasures. It's worth at least one visit to check out what they've got in your areas of interest. Or access their catalogues from your university online catalogue. Ask a reference librarian for help if you need to.

Keep your eyes open for any fliers advertising competitions for winning a voucher at the university bookshop, or getting a textbook bursary. These come up from time to time, and it's always worth entering the draw. If you can't see any notices around, ask your student union and your bookshop if they have any freebies of this nature planned for the near future.

OTHER EXPENSES

Books aside, what other expenses are you likely to encounter, and how can you cut corners?

Once the semester begins, you may be given lists of journal articles to read as tutorial and essay preparation. It's very tempting to simply photocopy every article each week, without looking closely at the material first. Try getting into the habit of glancing through the article before you photocopy it. It may be enough to take brief notes and put the journal back on the shelf.

The dangers of automatically photocopying everything are twofold. First, it's not always necessary, especially if the article proves to be of limited value. Second, it's very easy to let that pile of photocopies build up, unread, in a corner. This can bring on a major panic attack a week before exams when you realise that you've been meaning to read all those photocopies and never actually got around to it in time. What a waste of money!

Stationery is another expense which can blow your budget. Some people go way over the top, buying far too much stationery because it makes them feel more organised. You can spot these people in the bookshop staggering under teetering towers of new pens and paper, files, notebooks, highlighters, sticky notes and index cards. If you can afford it and it makes you feel extra-organised and ready to face the year, by all means stock up. If you're feeling the financial pinch, however, try a different approach. Only buy the stationery items you really need. Do you really need pens in five different colours? And how many highlighters can you use in one lifetime? Start out with the basics and work from there. A couple of notebooks, pens, pencils and files are a good beginning, and you can always build up your supplies as it becomes obvious that you need them.

What about the cost of buying a computer? If you already have one, great—you're at a distinct advantage. Most tutors these days prefer to receive assignments and essays which have been word-processed. In this electronic information age, you may as well get to grips with the basics of computers. It will make you more employable, and once you know how to drive one, a word-processing program can save you heaps of time and help you to produce better work.

If you can't afford to buy a computer, make some enquiries into the facilities available on campus. All universities have computer labs set up. These rooms are stocked with computers and printers which are available for use by students. There's normally a supervisor or lab manager available to help you out should you run into any problems. On-campus computing facilities for enrolled students are either free or cost very little. The resources are there; all you need to do is access them.

AVOIDING DEBT

Keep track of where your money goes. If you suddenly find yourself out of money and just can't account for where it went, try keeping a money notebook. Jot down where you spend your money from day to day. If you notice that most of it goes on takeaways, or going out, then you can make the necessary changes to your lifestyle and still have money in your wallet the day before payday. But you won't know what to cut back on without tracking your expenses first.

Did you know that you often don't have to pay your phone and electricity accounts all at once? Most of the time, you can arrange to part-pay a bill, say over two paydays. All you have to do is ring and negotiate some terms. But call as soon as you get the bill—it's much harder to bargain when your bill is already three weeks overdue.

It may surprise you to discover that the university library can be the source of an unexpected expense. Many university libraries will charge you for lost or overdue books. It's a good idea to keep track of when your books are due back at the library—and, unless you want to hand over a good chunk of your next Austudy payment, try not to leave any library books on the bus.

Make sure you don't let debt overwhelm you. If you're worried that you have rising debt and no way in sight of getting it under control, get some trusted advice immediately. In worst-case scenarios, it may be necessary to defer your studies or change your enrolment to part-time so that you can free up enough time to earn some money. Speak to a university counsellor if you're feeling panicky about your money situation. He or she may be able to help you, or refer you to someone else who can. Don't bear this burden on your own: there are plenty of people who can help ease the load—just pick up the phone and get in touch with one of them.

OTHER MONEY-SAVING IDEAS

- Save your coins (particularly the gold ones) in one place. This can be a great source of emergency funds when your next Austudy payment is still a few days away. But make sure you stockpile your coins in a well-hidden place; if someone breaks into your house, you'll be handing the thieves your money. You may think moneyboxes are for five-year-olds, but it's truly amazing how fast your change can build up. In the end, it's all legal tender—who cares whether it's in paper or coin form?

- If you're cooking for yourself or for your household and you end up with leftovers, put them into an airtight container and stick them in the freezer. Often leftovers get thrown out after being left to grow a thick covering of mould in the fridge for a week or two. But if you freeze them straight away, you have a ready-made meal that only needs to be defrosted and reheated. Why waste prepared food when you can turn it into an extra meal a week or two later?

- In extreme weather conditions, go in to university and work in the library. This will save you the cost of heating or cooling appliances and the energy they use. In addition, this strategy will bring you into contact with other students, and will also have the positive result of making it easier for you to study.

- In every transaction you make, check to see if there's a student discount. You can end up paying considerably less in your daily life if you're aware of every financial advantage there is to being a student. And always find out whether there's a free version of what you're looking for.

10. BEWARE THE QUICKSAND— EMERGENCY RESCUE TECHNIQUES

Once you've made it three-quarters of the way through your first year, you may find that the days are starting to fly by. The end of the year is moving steadily towards you, but you still have a few pieces of assessment to turn in. At this point, the sense of relief you feel in anticipation of finishing may be mingled with feelings of terror, as you find that you still have a lot of work to do but not much time to do it in. And your awareness of this mounting pressure won't be helped by the knowledge that exams are also just around the corner.

First of all, DON'T PANIC!

If you're worrying about passing your exams, go back and read Chapter 5 again. You'll find a comprehensive battle strategy for winning the exam fight there. In the meantime, let's examine some of the hidden dangers at university. We need to explore some techniques for thinking clearly under pressure, and realigning your strategy so that you get everything finished on time—and preferably without having a nervous breakdown!

MANAGING MULTIPLE OVERDUE ESSAYS

Problem: You have multiple essays due at the same time, and you haven't started to work on them early enough.

This is a very, very common problem, especially in first year, as it takes time to learn how to juggle a dozen things at once and take control of your time. So what can you do?

Solution:

- Remember that if you hand *something* in you're likely to get *some* marks for the assignment. But if you decide not to bother at all, you can guarantee you'll get a zero for that part of the assessment. And in some cases, not handing in work can get you kicked out of the unit altogether. It's always worth at least making an attempt at an assignment: the fact that you handed something in can mean the difference between a pass and a fail.

- Make a commitment of time for each outstanding assignment. Work out how much time you can devote to each, bearing in mind their weightings in terms of marks. Let's say you have three assignments: the first is worth 40 per cent of your final grade, the second is worth 15 per cent and the third is worth 5 per cent. Obviously you should spend the greatest part of your available time on the assignment worth the most marks. Once you've apportioned your time, don't deviate from this timetable.

- Clear your calendar of other activities. If you're under time pressure with essays, it's essential to get right back to basics. Nights at the pub and shopping expeditions will have to wait. If you find it hard to make these kinds of sacrifices, just ask yourself, 'Do I want to fail these units? Do I want to repeat them next year?' That will usually do the trick and get you focused. Remember, you only have to postpone your outside commitments until the assignments are due; you don't have to give up all hope of a social life forever.

- Go back over your lecture and tute notes for the topic you'll be working on. Use the ideas you find there as a jumping-off point for some intensive further research. Keep things simple and focused: work out which information you still need to find, and map out the main points you'll be covering in your essay. Refer once again to the guidelines in Chapter 4 if you're unclear about the requirements and basic structure of a university essay.

- Keep your research to essentials only. If you have a limited amount of time to read *and* write, you'll need to move fast and absorb only what you can incorporate effectively into your essay. If the essay deadline is very near, there's a good chance that the best secondary reading will already have been borrowed from the library anyway, so there'll be a limit to what you can get your hands on to read. The essential reading will probably be in Closed Reserve, though, and journal articles cannot be borrowed, so they will also be available to you. Avoid the temptation to base your entire assignment on information you find on the internet or the simplistic information you'll find in encyclopedias (see Chapter 3 on research). Refer instead to the reading lists given out during the course and follow the recommended texts. Demonstrating that you have a basic grasp of the essential ideas in the course will get you some marks.

- If you're low on information and you know your argument could be stronger, take a few minutes before you hand in your essay to pay attention to the details of presentation. Run the spell-check function through the document and proofread your work properly by reading it out loud to yourself. Make sure that all necessary footnotes are included, and a bibliography is also attached. Do what you can to indicate that you respect the rigours of the discipline and are working to conform with them.

How to avoid this problem in future:

It's a fact that if you leave everything to the last minute, you not only make it much harder for yourself to get decent marks but you also make the university experience stressful instead of exciting and stimulating. The way to avoid this danger is to refine your time-management skills, and to replace procrastination with action.

WHAT TO DO WHEN YOUR TUTOR HATES YOU

Problem: You haven't made it to many tutes and you're pretty sure you haven't made a good impression on your tutor.

This is a tricky one. If you've missed a lot of tutorials and haven't established much of a connection with your tutor, it's a bit late to start from scratch at this stage in the year. This can be a fairly serious problem in units where tutorial participation and attendance actually make up a percentage of your final grade. But there are still a couple of things you can do.

Bear in mind that your tutor has heard every excuse and sob-story ever told. Think up the most outrageous and imaginative excuse for missing tutes you can, and I can guarantee your tutor has either already heard the exact same story or some variation of it. So it won't help to waste half an hour of your tutor's time with an elaborate explanation as to why you've missed so many tutes. Actions, not words are more likely to make a difference.

Solution (if you have a legitimate excuse for having missed tutorials):
- Your tutor will be more accommodating if you make contact and discuss the nature of your problem as soon as it develops. You may have been sick or had serious personal or family problems. If you have medical certificates or other documentation explaining your absences, it's worth your while making an appointment to see your tutor and discussing your options.

- Speak to your tutor about deferring assessment and exams. There may be a way of being granted special consideration for your circumstances, which can result in you being allowed to sit later exams or hand in late assignments. Be aware, though, that it's doubly hard to get motivated once the unit is officially over and all your friends are celebrating having survived the year.

Solution (if you don't have a proper reason for having missed tutorials):
- Turn up to the rest of the tutes for the year. Do whatever you have to do to get there. Make sure you've done the reading and are ready to

talk about it with the group. You'll make some kind of positive impression on your tutor, even at this late stage, if you demonstrate that you can be a productive member of the learning group. And, if this unit includes tutorial participation and attendance as part of your final mark, some marks are better than no marks at all.

- It may be worth getting to the first of the remaining tutes a few minutes early, to introduce yourself to your tutor and offer some brief but sincere words of apology for missing so much of the course. Don't try to justify your absence; simply explain that you'd like to try and get what you can out of the rest of the course. Nine times out of ten, tutors appreciate a bit of sincerity. And if you do get a bit of a dressing-down, try to take it with good grace.

How to avoid this problem in future:
You only have to find yourself in this situation once to realise how easily it could have been avoided. Make an effort in the future to attend the majority of your tutes, and see your tutor immediately if you're falling behind or if you have a good reason for being unable to attend. Tutors respond most positively to enthusiastic and organised students, so do what you can to fit into this category. Never forget that these are the people who have the final say on your mark for the whole semester or year. Stay on their good side if you possibly can.

WHAT IF YOUR RESEARCH NOTES ARE IN DISARRAY?
Problem: Your lecture notes and photocopies of articles are scattered all over your house, in no particular order.

This is evidence of the dangerous condition known as 'nonexistent filing system'. It's easily cured with a bit of time and effort. As you make order out of chaos, you'll be amazed at how much less stressed you feel. Suddenly you'll know where to find information about everything you've studied so far this semester. It's a great sensation of relief.

Solution:

- Come to grips with the fact that you need to set aside a block of time—probably two or three hours—to get things in order. Don't kid yourself that you can get to it later. At this stage in the year the pressure only increases, so do it now and you'll really appreciate your efforts when the exam-preparation schedule starts kicking in.

- Assemble the essential tools: several lever-arch files, some file dividers, felt-tip pens, a hole punch and a stapler. It's not enough to make temporary piles on your desk or kitchen floor. They only get messed up again, and you can waste an unlimited amount of time if you have to go through this process repeatedly.

- Clear yourself a large working space—the kitchen table or living-room floor is fine. Grab a pile of disorganised papers and start rough-sorting them into the different units you're doing. Once you've done this for all the piles of paper you have stacked around the place, recover with a short break. Then start tackling one pile at a time, fine-sorting them into topics within the unit, or into weekly chunks of information.

- When you have 'sub-piles' for your first unit, get out one of your lever-arch files and slot the papers in the separate piles into their own topic sections. Use your file dividers and make sure you label each subdivision clearly with a felt-tip pen. Label the files themselves too, along the spine, so that you can save time in future by going straight to the relevant file for each unit.

- Make some space for your new filing system. Keep your files together, in an accessible area, so you can get to them whenever you need them.

How to avoid this problem in future:

If you set up this kind of simple filing system at the beginning of the year, it's pretty easy to get into the habit of filing your notes, handouts and photocopies in the right place as soon as you've finished writing or reading them. That way, you save yourself half a day of filing at a time when you're already stressed by the pressure of many deadlines, and you can cruise through the semester with a calm feeling of being in control of your information. It's a very reassuring position to be in.

STAYING SANE WHEN YOU LIVE WITH PARTY ANIMALS

Problem: Your living arrangements are interfering with your ability to study.

You might have discovered too late that you're sharing a house with people who'd rather motor through a carton of beer than hit the books. Or maybe you're living with family members who can't seem to comprehend your need for separate study space and some quiet, uninterrupted time. What can you do if you don't want to go to the pub five times a week, or cook dinner for three other people every night?

Solution:

- If the relationship is still on a civil footing, the first step is to talk to everyone involved about your needs. Make it into a formal discussion rather than a passing chat. Call a house meeting and get everyone sitting down together around the kitchen table. Let the other members of your household know that you're worried about being able to find the time and energy to study, given the current living conditions. Ask them for their help and support and let them know how important it is for you to get your degree. You may be pleasantly surprised: in many cases, other people are simply unaware of what's required for successful study, especially if they haven't ever been to university themselves. Come to a new agreement about how the household will work from now on.

- Sometimes it helps to have some written notes to keep you on track during this meeting. Make a list of what you need, and also suggestions about how you can achieve it. For example, if the cooking or cleaning needs to be shared out more evenly, make up a sample roster and run it by the other members of the household. Ask if you can rotate some of the chores so that you have more spare time when you have assignments due. Keep things friendly and calm and ask for everyone's ideas. Note them down, and go over the conclusions you reach to make sure that everyone agrees on what's been decided.

- If you try these rational approaches and find that nothing changes, you may have to take more radical action. It might be necessary to stay somewhere else for a couple of weeks so that you have the time and space to get all your work completed on time. Ask your more understanding friends or your family whether you can stay with them temporarily until you sort out your current living arrangements.

- The worst-case scenario will involve you moving out permanently, or asking a difficult housemate to move out. This is enormously stressful and time-consuming and has real potential to derail your whole semester. If it's humanly possible, put off taking this kind of action until after exams, when you have the time and energy to devote to finding a new place to live, or different people to share with.

How to avoid this problem in future:
Now that you know first-hand that studying involves sustained focus and some peace and quiet, it'll be easier to custom-fit your environment to your needs. If you're moving into a different place, or just renegotiating the rules of your current home, make sure that you communicate your needs clearly and firmly to the other members of the household. Never let anyone make you feel that your need for a pleasant and peaceful study environment is unreasonable: it's your degree and your future that are at stake.

FOUR MORE DANGEROUS SITUATIONS AND HOW TO ESCAPE THEM

As you've seen, making your way around Planet University requires you to learn some tricky survival skills—and pretty quickly, too. Here are a few more of the common snares you might find yourself caught in at university. While it's usually possible to escape them, it's always easier to avoid these traps in the first place. Here's what to look out for and what to do if you find yourself in a dangerous predicament.

Trap 1: You feel threatened (sexually or physically) by another student, or even by a tutor.

How to escape:

Make an immediate appointment to see an authority figure you trust. Each campus has sexual discrimination officers who are there to stamp out this kind of intimidation on campus.

You can also speak to a student union representative, university counsellor, lecturer or tutor about your fears. Don't put up with this kind of treatment, and don't wait to do something about it. Protect yourself now, before the behaviour goes any further.

Trap 2: You feel you've been unfairly treated by a tutor, either in tutes or in the assessment of your written work.

How to escape:

There's a certain process you should go through in this situation. If at all possible, speak to your tutor first about the problem. If this doesn't help, go to the head of the department or school. Most problems can be sorted out at this level. If not, the relevant head can advise you on the avenues of appeal open to you.

Be aware, though, that this is a fairly radical route to take. While you should never tolerate unfair treatment, there's a fine line between making sure that justice is done and getting a name as a troublemaker in your department. Take some time to think calmly about the situation and consider whether you have it in perspective. Seek the advice of a more experienced person about the best thing you should do before making any extreme moves you may later regret.

Trap 3: Finding that an ex-boyfriend or ex-girlfriend, or someone else you no longer speak to, has turned up in your tute group.

How to escape:
Think about the possibility of changing your tutorial group. Check the available times and talk to your tutor about whether you can attend a different tute. Don't go into the details of why you broke up with the person in question, or why you're no longer on speaking terms with that guy in the corner. Simply explain that you've had personal differences in the past and feel uncomfortable about being in the same tutorial with this person. This is a perfectly reasonable request, and your tutor will probably try to accommodate you.

If it's *not* possible to get into a different tute, you'll just have to accept it and be civil to this person, at least within the timeframe of the tute. It sometimes happens that you have personality clashes with people in your tutes anyway, so just think of this as one of those times. Avoid getting into a public slanging match. This sort of behaviour will destabilise the whole tute and probably negatively affect your mark.

Trap 4: Studying costs more than you ever imagined, and you're having a serious financial crisis that may cause you to drop out of university.

How to escape:
Talk to someone who can help you put the problem in perspective. Everyone who goes to university has at least one (and more likely several) panic attacks about money, unless they're from a very wealthy family. There is almost always a way around the problem. Speak to your family about an emergency short-term loan, think about extending your credit limit (and then get a holiday job to start paying the money

back as soon as possible!), or talk to your student union about loans or scholarships. The university counsellor is also a good person to see about this problem; he or she may be able to advise you on the best course of action to take for your individual circumstances.

In the meantime, do what you can to make it to the end of semester or year so that you don't waste all the hard work you've put in so far. Unfortunately it's just a fact of life that education costs money, but if you're working hard and really engaging with your course, it'll be well worth the investment.

CONCLUSIONS:

REVIEWING YOUR YEAR

When you make it to the end of the year, pause for a moment of self-assessment. How did you do? Take some time to actually consider the high and low points of your year. Chances are you've discovered some new things about yourself and your talents. What are you good at? And what do you need to work on for next year?

After a year's worth of effort, it's essential that you take some time to relax and recover. Think about how it will feel to wake up in the morning and realise that no assignments are due, and that you don't have to make it to any lectures. Use this breathing space to regenerate your mental and physical batteries. Catch up with people you may have neglected in the lead-up to exams and end-of-year assignments, and reward yourself for making it through a scary period of adjustment. If you can afford it (or if someone else is willing to pay!), grab the opportunity for some time away. Or organise to have drinks with new or old friends to mark the end of study. Having some kind of ritual to mark the end of year is a great way to separate yourself from the university challenges you've been dealing with for so many months.

The period between semesters or years is the perfect time to iron out any problems which may have appeared so far. Do you need to sort out your living arrangements? Or maybe you could arrange to work some extra hours at your part-time job to shore up your finances? Take a look at your life and see what needs to be fine-tuned. As you've now discovered, it's very difficult to deal with extra stress when you're in the middle of writing assignments and doing mountains of reading! Solve any persistent problems *now*.

If you have some idea of the required reading for next year, why not get a jump on this material by checking it out in advance? Drop into the library and start doing some exploring. Sure, you may feel like a bit of a nerd as you browse the stacks in the peace and quiet of the summer break, but you'll be way ahead of the competition come the beginning of the new year. Wouldn't it be great to face next year's challenges feeling confident rather than disoriented?

Congratulations on making it through the first, and most daunting part of your degree! Building on the new skills you've already learned, it only gets easier from here on in. A university education can open the doors to worlds you haven't even imagined. But, as well as expanding your options for the future, it also offers you the opportunity to embark on a unique and stimulating process of self-discovery. So what if you have to sit through the odd tedious lecture and give an occasional nerve-wracking tutorial presentation? It will all be worth it when you hold your degree in your hand and find that somehow you just can't seem to stop smiling.

APPENDIX: USEFUL CONTACTS

For information on Austudy, Abstudy and Youth Allowance, contact:
Centrelink
Tel: 13 24 90
www.centrelink.gov.au

For information on course fees, contact:
HECS
Tel: 1800 020 108
www.hecs.gov.au

To find your nearest Tertiary Admissions Centre, visit:
www.careers.gov.au/tertiary_education_01.htm

Useful Australian job search web sites:
www.jobsearch.gov.au
www.careersonline.com.au
www.employment.com.au
www.gradlink.edu.au/gradlink/studfrm.htm
www.graduate.com.au
www.graduateopportunities.com
www.campus.monster.com.au
www.mycareer.com.au
www.positionsvacant.com.au
www.webwombat.com.au/jobs

ACKNOWLEDGMENTS

I am grateful to the following people, who have all made valuable contributions to this project.

My family have provided ongoing support and encouragement: Audrey, Richard and Mary Hardy; Rebecca and Cameron McNeilage; Dylan and Tess Wheatley.

The members of my extended family have also been unfailingly positive and enthusiastic: Melanie Arundale; Martin Drum; Channa Galhenage; Bruce Hunt; Henry Jackson; Paul Laffey; Kirsten and Ross Lambert; Simon Malloch; Anna Molyneux; Patsy Primozich; Ed Scully; Mike Smith.

A special thank you to Van Ikin and Toby Burrows, for their important roles in my own university experience.

Sophie Church and Anouska Good generously offered insightful editorial guidance and suggestions.

And thank you to Pat Wheatley, for his part in this book and a million other acts of faith.

INDEX

NOTES

Use these blank pages to make your own survival notes and to keep a
record of any useful contacts you make.